YOU CAN CREATE AN *exceptional* LIFE

ALSO BY LOUISE HAY

BOOKS/KIT

All Is Well (with Mona Lisa Schulz, M.D.)
Colors & Numbers
Empowering Women
Everyday Positive Thinking
Experience Your Good Now! (book-with-audio)
A Garden of Thoughts: My Affirmation Journal
Gratitude: A Way of Life (Louise & Friends)
Heal Your Body
Heal Your Body A–Z
Heart Thoughts (also available in a gift edition)
I Can Do It® (book-with-audio)
Inner Wisdom
Letters to Louise
Life! Reflections on Your Journey
Love Your Body
Love Yourself, Heal Your Life Workbook
Meditations to Heal Your Life (also available in a gift edition)
Modern-Day Miracles (Louise & Friends)
The Power Is Within You
Power Thoughts
The Present Moment
The Times of Our Lives (Louise & Friends)
You Can Heal Your Heart (with David Kessler)
You Can Heal Your Life (also available in a gift edition)
You Can Heal Your Life Affirmation Kit
You Can Heal Your Life Companion Book

FOR CHILDREN

The Adventures of Lulu
I Think, I Am! (with Kristina Tracy)
Lulu and the Ant: A Message of Love
Lulu and the Dark: Conquering Fears
Lulu and Willy the Duck: Learning Mirror Work

AUDIO PROGRAMS

All Is Well (audio book)
Anger Releasing
Cancer
Change and Transition
Dissolving Barriers
Embracing Change
The Empowering Women Gift Collection
Feeling Fine Affirmations
Forgiveness/Loving the Inner Child
How to Love Yourself
Meditations for Personal Healing
Meditations to Heal Your Life (audio book)
Morning and Evening Meditations
101 Power Thoughts
Overcoming Fears
The Power Is Within You (audio book)
The Power of Your Spoken Word
Receiving Prosperity
Self-Esteem Affirmations (subliminal)
Self-Healing
Stress-Free (subliminal)
Totality of Possibilities
What I Believe and Deep Relaxation
You Can Heal Your Heart (audio book)
You Can Heal Your Life (audio book)
You Can Heal Your Life Study Course
Your Thoughts Create Your Life

DVDs

Dissolving Barriers
Receiving Prosperity
You Can Heal Your Life Study Course
You Can Heal Your Life, THE MOVIE
(also available in an expanded edition)
You Can Trust Your Life (with Cheryl Richardson)

CARD DECKS

Healthy Body Cards
I Can Do It® Cards
I Can Do It® Cards . . . for Creativity, Forgiveness, Health, Job Success, Wealth, Romance
Power Thought Cards
Power Thoughts for Teens
Power Thought Sticky Cards
Wisdom Cards

CALENDAR

I Can Do It® Calendar (for each individual year)

and

THE LOUISE HAY BOOK COLLECTION
(comprising the gift versions of *Meditations to Heal Your Life, You Can Heal Your Life,* and *You Can Heal Your Life Companion Book*)

All of the above are available at your local bookstore, or may be ordered by visiting:

Hay House USA: **www.hayhouse.com®**
Hay House Australia: **www.hayhouse.com.au**
Hay House UK: **www.hayhouse.co.uk**
Hay House India: **www.hayhouse.co.in**

Louise's websites: **www.LouiseHay.com®** and **www.HealYourLife.com®**

ALSO BY CHERYL RICHARDSON

BOOKS

*The Art of Extreme Self-Care**
Take Time for Your Life
Life Makeovers
The Unmistakable Touch of Grace
Stand Up for Your Life
*Turning Inward**

AUDIO PROGRAMS

*The Art of Extreme Self-Care**
Take Time for Your Life
*Stand Up for Your Life**
*Create an Abundant Life**
*Finding Your Passion**
*Tuning In**
*Experience the Power of Grace**

CARD DECKS

My Daily Affirmation Cards (a 50-card deck)*
Grace Cards (a 50-card deck)*
Self-Care Cards (a 52-card deck)*

*Available from Hay House

YOU CAN CREATE AN *exceptional* LIFE

Louise Hay
and
Cheryl Richardson

HAY HOUSE

HAY HOUSE INDIA
New Delhi • London • Sydney
Carlsbad, California • New York City

Hay House Publishers (India) Pvt Ltd
Muskaan Complex, Plot No. 3, B-2, Vasant Kunj, New Delhi – 110070, India

Hay House LLC, P.O. Box 5100, Carlsbad, CA 92018-5100, USA
Hay House UK Ltd, 1st Floor, Crawford Corner, 91-93 Baker Street, London W1U 6QQ, UK
Hay House Australia Publishing Pty Ltd, 18/36 Ralph St., Alexandria NSW 2015, Australia

Email: contact@hayhouse.co.in
Website: www.hayhouse.co.in

Editorial supervision: Jill Kramer • *Project editor:* Shannon Littrell
Cover design: Christy Salinas • *Interior design:* Nick C. Welch

First published by Hay House India, 2011
Reprint, 2026
24 23 22 21 20 19 18 17 16 15

ISBN 978-93-81431-09-2

Printed at Repro India Limited

MIX
Paper from responsible sources
FSC® C047271

Hay House is committed to a sustainable future for our business, our readers and our planet. This book is made from Forest Stewardship Council® certified paper.

CONTENTS

Introduction

by Louise Hay

For many years one of my affirmations has been: *Only good lies before me.* It is a comforting thought that wipes out all fear of the future and allows me to wake up each day with confidence, feeling at ease. I am often delighted and even amazed to observe how Life brings my next good adventure to me.

That is how I felt when I heard that Reid Tracy, the CEO of Hay House, was cooking up a scheme to have Cheryl and me produce a book together. A huge smile lit up my face as the idea penetrated my consciousness with possibilities.

At first, I had many questions: What would we write about? How would we blend our two styles? Since we live so far apart, would Life give us enough together time? But soon I realized that Life could not have come up with such a good idea without covering all the bases. And cover the bases it did. Cheryl and I found ourselves in various cities, both here and abroad, with the perfect amount of time to lay out a chapter or two. And when we weren't together, we would Skype—often in our pajamas, with our hair and makeup au naturel—and it was as if we were in the same room.

Cheryl and I have both made phenomenally positive changes in our lives, and we want to share what we've learned with you. All of us can improve the quality of our lives if we practice the art of self-care and train our minds to think thoughts that make us feel good. When we do, we attract delightful experiences that enrich our lives.

The idea Cheryl and I had was to present these methods in the easiest possible way so that you could, step-by-step, learn how to have peace of mind—to live worry free in a healthy body, with a comfortable income, while enjoying your relationships. Ultimately, we wanted to show you how to move from feeling like a victim to being the creator of an enjoyable life.

As you read this book chapter by chapter, you will notice your shoulders relaxing, your brow lines smoothing out, and your tension and fearfulness dissolving as you realize that there is a better way to live.

It is the journey that brings pleasure, not the race to a destination. We love you and support you as you move with us on this great new adventure toward an exceptional life!

Introduction

by Cheryl Richardson

There is a Universal energy, a Divine force that creates us; sustains us; connects us to one another; and works in cooperation with our thoughts, words, and actions to generate our life experiences. When we recognize and learn to work in partnership with this benevolent power, we become masters of our own destiny. The formula is simple: *Think thoughts that make you feel good, make choices that make you feel good, and take actions that make you feel good.* Then surrender the outcome, trusting that Life will bring you what you need to grow and be happy.

This simple formula has radically improved the quality of my life, and it can improve yours, too. When you use it, and learn to trust it, life unfolds in miraculous ways. You'll be presented with extraordinary opportunities to make your life whole and to make a difference in the world. This book is one of my extraordinary opportunities.

It was late afternoon as I sat down to have lunch with Reid Tracy, the CEO of Hay House. Reid and I have known each other for many years, and recently we'd been teaching a workshop for experienced professionals who wanted to learn how to expand their reach. Together, we walk participants through the process of writing and publishing, public speaking, appearing on radio and television, and using social media to build an audience for their work. We call the workshop *Speak, Write & Promote: Become a Mover & Shaker;* and it's a legacy project that affords us the privilege of cultivating new, conscious leaders in the self-empowerment field.

As we began eating our lunch and discussing the progress of our latest workshop, Reid caught me off guard with an unexpected invitation: "I've been thinking about your next project, and I wonder if you'd be interested in writing a book with Louise."

I carefully placed my fork on the table next to my plate, and looked up at him. "Louise Hay?" I asked with a mouth full of food and a worthy amount of surprise.

"Yes," he said with a smile, "Louise Hay."

Louise is considered one of the founders of the self-help movement and a pioneer in mind-body healing, and I'd known her for more than 20 years. Not personally, in the beginning, but through her writing and speaking. Published in 1984, her book *You Can Heal Your Life* was one of the first to introduce the connection between physical ailments and their corresponding thought patterns and emotional issues. I knew that Louise's books have sold more than 50 million copies and that people from all over the world have been influenced by her work.

As I sat staring at Reid, the phrase *coming full circle* popped into my head. Write with Louise Hay? My mind flashed back to our first meeting. It was the mid-1980s, and I was a young woman trying to find myself. *You Can Heal Your Life* was one of the first books to set me on my own healing path.

At the time I was volunteering at a place called Interface in Cambridge, Massachusetts. Interface was a holistic education center that boasted a curriculum taught by cutting-edge thinkers such as Marion Woodman, a Jungian analyst and pioneer of feminine psychology; John Bradshaw, the man who introduced the concept of dysfunctional families to America through his PBS series *Bradshaw On: The Family;* and Bernie

Siegel, the surgeon who challenged doctors and patients to see healing as a holistic process that encompassed our emotional and spiritual lives, as well as our physical bodies. Louise was set to give a lecture about her book at Interface, and I had been chosen to drive her from the airport to her hotel.

The thought of picking up Louise Hay at the airport was exciting. I was both anxious and thrilled to meet someone who had touched my life so deeply. In her book, Louise told the intimate story of her life with such courage and vulnerability that she felt like a kindred spirit. Her ability to turn a violent, abusive past into a present filled with peace and healing inspired me to get on a healthy path myself. And she challenged me to see growth from a radically new perspective: If I wanted to change my own life, I first needed to change my thinking. No more victim of circumstance. It was time for me to step firmly into the driver's seat by using the practical tools she provided to make positive, long-lasting changes.

As I drove to the airport, I had to keep reminding myself to keep my excitement in check, avoid bombarding her with questions, and give her plenty of space. When I arrived, I discovered that her flight from California had been delayed, so I sat at the gate for more than two hours and my excitement never waned.

It grew. Eventually, when Louise stepped off the plane, I made my way up to the gateway and introduced myself. She smiled and shook my hand, and then we walked to the car. I barely said a word all the way to the hotel.

Life would bring us together again several years later—this time under very different circumstances. The young girl who was so desperate to find herself in the '80s became a woman who would write books and take others on their own journey of self-discovery. This time, Louise and I would meet again at an authors' dinner hosted by her publishing company, Hay House. This would be the first of many meetings that would allow us to get to know each other in a more personal—and meaningful—way.

As the years passed, our time together provided me with a refreshing look at someone who, even now, at the age of 84, still practices—*diligently*—what she teaches. Louise is a beautiful example of what it means to think and speak your way to an exceptional life.

Now, as I considered Reid's idea, my first thought was, *This would be a unique opportunity to learn from a woman who has had such a vast impact on my life as well as the lives of millions of others*. It was a no-brainer. I'd write the book for the experience alone. There was more, however. My life was still being influenced in significant ways by the wisdom of Louise's work.

Over the previous year, for instance, I'd maintained a daily practice inspired by her teachings on affirmations. Each morning before starting my day, I'd write a few pages in my journal and finish with a list of spontaneous affirmations. I looked forward to this new ritual and was curious about how it might influence my life.

No sooner had I embarked on this practice than I began to notice tangible changes. I felt better throughout the day; I had more enthusiasm for life; and I found it easier to shift my mind away from things that irritated or upset me to thoughts that made me feel good. Not only that, but the longer I continued this daily practice, the more I was able to recognize deeper, more personal needs. Within months, I began to see patterns and themes in the affirmations I was creating. Certain ones would show up over and over again, alerting me to experiences I yearned to draw into my life. One, in particular, kept taking center stage:

I work in creative collaboration with smart, inspiring people on projects that contribute to the healing of the world.

At first, this affirmation surprised me. A lone ranger by nature—well, a control freak, really—I preferred to be in charge and call all the shots. But this was becoming a lonely, less satisfying way to operate in the world. I was beginning to think more about working with others who challenged and inspired me rather than moving through life alone. Now, I watched as Life made it clear it was paying attention. The power of focusing my energy was manifesting something new.

As I thought more about Reid's invitation, I made a decision to walk through the open door before me. "Yes, I would love to write a book with Louise," I told him. "What's the next step?"

Weeks later, Louise and I met to discuss working together. We agreed that writing a book was a great idea, and we decided to do something only age and experience could inspire: *Trust Life*. Rather than create an outline or follow some kind of organized plan, she and I would allow the book to reveal itself. And reveal itself it did.

While attending events throughout North America and Europe, Louise and I enjoyed a series of intimate, heart-to-heart conversations about the spiritual principles that have shaped our lives. Although I've written the book from my point of view, it reflects our collaborative experience of talking about everything from loving ourselves and our bodies to the ways in which we've dealt with a variety of topics—including aging and a dignified, peaceful approach to the end of our lives here on Earth.

It is our sincere wish that these conversations inspire you to develop the spiritual habits that will support you in living an exceptional life. As you do, you'll soon discover what Louise and I know to be the most important universal truth of all: *Life loves you!*

CHAPTER ONE

Answer the Phone and Open the Mail

I'm at home in Massachusetts, looking out over a frozen landscape, getting ready to call Louise in sunny California. Next to my computer, I have a cup of my favorite tea—Fortnum & Mason's Royal Blend—mixed with the perfect amount of homemade, raw almond milk. I'm excited to get started on our project.

When we first scheduled our call, I was caught off guard when Louise suggested that we Skype so we could see each other while we talked. *Skype?* I thought. *Really?* I had only begun using the program myself a year earlier. Already I was learning how hip Louise is at 84 years old. This was going to be some ride.

In an effort to get to know Louise on a deeper level, and to begin to navigate my way through this project, I was anxious to hear about her personal journey. I wondered what prompted her to get on the self-empowerment path. What guideposts directed her along the way? What inspired her to create a company that has had such a profound impact on the lives of millions of people around the world?

My curiosity was tempered with some reservation, though. I knew Louise had shared her story many times before, both in *You Can Heal Your Life* as well as numerous talks and workshops. And, as someone who has written extensively about my own life, I know that it's a tedious telling the 400th time around. So I was determined to hear about her life from a new perspective. I was eager to learn about the wisdom gained from age and experience.

With what I would come to recognize as well-honed intuition, Louise addressed my concerns right up front as we scheduled our first time to talk. "I've already told my life story in my books, so I think it's unnecessary to go there again. I've been thinking about the things that are relevant to my spiritual growth, however, and I thought we could talk about that."

I took a deep breath and smiled. "Excellent," I told her. "That would be great."

At the appropriate hour, I dial Louise, click on the video button, and we are connected. There she is!

Beaming smile, glasses perched high on her nose, sitting upright in her chair, and clearly ready for business. After chatting for a few minutes, we get to work. I set my iPhone to record, place my fingers on the keyboard of my computer so I can take notes, and listen carefully as Louise considers my first question: *What prompted you to get on the spiritual path?*

"My spiritual growth started when I was around 42," she begins. "I had been married to a delightful Englishman who had given me the opportunity to learn the social graces, manners, and ways of operating in the world that had been missing from my childhood. I grew up in a violent family, and we never went anywhere or did anything. I ran away from home at 15, and while I did learn survival skills, I had no skills for living well in the world. So, when I married this man who was very worldly and had the best of manners, I learned a lot from him. We did all sorts of wonderful things together, and just as I was telling myself that good things can last and we'd probably be together forever, he told me he wanted a divorce. I was shattered."

My goodness, that must have been awful, I tell her.

"Yes. My husband was a prominent person, and our divorce was all over the newspapers. It was a very painful time because I immediately told myself, 'See, once again, you can't do anything right.' But when I look back now, I see that the marriage was an important door that needed to close in order for me to move toward the next step on my pathway. If I had not been divorced, I would never have become this Louise Hay. Instead, I would have stayed the dutiful little English wife—a very good wife according to my concept of it, but not who I was meant to be. It was time for it to end."

As I listen to Louise, I think about the classic wake-up call, the often-abrupt and unexpected rupture that can occur in a comfortably numb life. I certainly had my share of these before I finally started to wake up—gut-wrenching heartbreaks, the shame of being fired from a job, and an actual fire that destroyed our family business. In fact, it was that fire that ultimately brought me out of my deep sleep and planted me firmly on the spiritual path.

"It was a year later, after dealing with the loss of my marriage, that a new door opened," Louise continues. "I had a friend who invited me to a lecture at a Church of Religious Science in New York. She asked me to join her because she didn't want to go by herself. I agreed, but when I arrived, she wasn't there. I was left to decide whether or not to attend by myself, and I decided to stay. So there I was, sitting in this lecture, when I heard someone say, 'If you are willing to change your thinking, you can change your life.' While it sounded like a small, tiny statement, it was huge to me. It caught my attention."

Why do you think that caught your attention? I ask her.

"I have no idea, because I was a person who never studied anything. I remember having a friend who kept trying to get me to go to the YWCA for classes, and I wasn't interested. But something about this subject spoke to me at that time, and I made a decision to go back. I can now see the perfection in my friend not showing up. If she had, I probably would have had a different experience. You see, everything is perfect."

Everything is perfect. At first, hearing this phrase is like hearing that everything happens for a reason. It's a tough message to swallow when faced with tragedy or deep pain of any kind. But, by training ourselves to see the perfection in our most difficult moments—a perspective that can often only be seen in hindsight—we learn to trust Life. We come to understand that, while we might not like a certain outcome, Life may be leading us in a new, more appropriate and beneficial direction.

Everything happens for a reason or *Everything is perfect* are beliefs born from a decision to see life as a schoolroom. When we choose to become students of life who learn and grow from our experiences, everything does, in fact, happen for a reason. In this way, we make our most difficult moments mean something by using them to our spiritual advantage.

Louise goes on. "After that first talk I started to attend lectures at the church regularly. I wanted to learn more. I discovered that they had a yearlong training program, so I made a decision to become a student and enrolled. I didn't even have the book at the first training, so I just listened. Then I took the entire training program again—this time with the book. It was a very slow beginning, but I stayed with it. Three years later, I was eligible to become one of their licensed practitioners, which meant I was able to do church counseling."

What exactly did a church counselor do?

"During these sessions, a person would come to me with a problem—an illness or financial hardship, for example—and I would do a 'treatment' with them. A treatment was our form of prayer. In this prayer we would acknowledge the fact that there is one Infinite Power, and we are part of this Intelligence. We would declare the truth—the outcome we wanted—in a positive way. For example: *My body is healthy and free from illness,* or *There is an unlimited supply of prosperity for my family and me.* Then we would end the prayer with 'So be it.' From that point on, when the person thought about the problem, they needed to use their fear or worry as a trigger to remind them to reaffirm that Life was taking care of it, and they were fine."

I was very familiar with the concept of conducting a treatment. In my mid-20s I was captivated by the writings of New Thought teachers such as Catherine Ponder, Florence Scovel Shinn, Norman Vincent Peale, and Robert Collier. And when I was in my early 30s, my best friend, Max, had given me a book by Dr. Emmet Fox, a New Thought minister, called *Sermon on the Mount*. This book radically changed my way of thinking and inspired me to study Fox's work more intensely. In fact, his *Power Through Constructive Thinking* became my manual for living for a year. I studied every word and put into practice his teachings about conducting treatments to tap into the Universal Source of Power available to us all.

"I love Emmet Fox," Louise says. "He was a very good man. I enjoyed his work very much and have used it continually in my own life."

Turning back to her work as a counselor, she tells me, "Once I finished my training and began working with people, I developed a following pretty quickly. Most church counselors did their work on the weekends or during evenings, but within three weeks I was doing it full-time. It was incredible. People were just drawn to me and wanted to work with me."

What do you make of that? Why so much so fast?

"I don't know. Ever since I first put my foot onto the spiritual pathway, I felt I had no control over anything, nor did I have to try to control anything. Life has always brought me what I needed. I've always just responded to what showed up. So often people ask about how I started Hay House. They want to know every detail from the day I began up to today. My answer is always the same: I answered the phone and opened the mail. I did what was before me."

I knew exactly what Louise was talking about. Although I'd been on my own spiritual path since my mid-20s, it wasn't until I hit my early 40s that I started *responding* to Life rather than always trying to direct it. In my 20s and 30s I was someone who took goal setting seriously. I made lists of career goals, financial goals, relationship goals, and so on; and I created action plans and treasure maps to support them. Looking back, they were wonderful tools that allowed me to harness my creative energy, but at some point things changed. Something shifted inside me. Although I still created treasure maps—visual boards or collages reflecting images that made me feel good and gave me something to aspire to—I became less interested in hunting for success and more concerned with how present I was to the direction Life was calling me to go in.

"That's how I lived," Louise continues. "It was as if Life simply took care of everything one step at a time. So the business started first with me and my then-90-year-old mother, who was very good at sealing envelopes and licking stamps, and it grew from there.

"When I look back, I can see how Life put exactly what I needed in my path. After my divorce, for example, I had a boyfriend who was a director. He was part of the Spanish/American Theater in New York, and I worked with him and some of the actors for about a year. It was experimental theater, and I ended up doing things I never thought of doing before. When this director went back to Spain, I stayed, and ended up performing in a play that allowed me to get my Actors' Equity card. From that moment on—from the moment I received my Equity card, which was a big deal—it all disappeared. No one called me, and no one wanted me. But because I hadn't gone into the theater wanting to make a career of it, I didn't care."

How was the theater an example of Life giving you what you needed?

"It was my preparation for the public speaking I would do later on. When I started speaking, it wasn't terrifying to me because I had already made an ass of myself on the stage. And people sort of liked it. What I realized was that public speaking was the same thing as theater, except I got to write my own script. I didn't have to do what someone else wanted me to do; I got to do what *I* wanted to do."

So you were working full-time as a counselor, and people just seemed to be drawn to you. How did your work evolve from there?

"One of the things we worked on at the 'School of Religious Science' (I call it a school) was diseases and the mental equivalents for them, and I was fascinated by this idea. I remember making notes—and at one point I put together a list of things I found in books, ideas that had come to me, and what I was seeing from the people I worked with, and I called it a list. I shared it with someone in my class, and the woman said, 'Louise, this is incredible! Why don't you make a pamphlet out of it?'

"So I put together this little pamphlet that was 12 pages long, and I put a blue cover around it. I titled it *What Hurts,* but eventually it would affectionately come to be known as 'the little blue book.' It contained a list of diseases, the mental patterns that may be contributing to each disease, and a short treatment to heal the negative patterns. I still remember going to Dr. Barker, the head of the school, and showing him what I had done. He said, 'Oh, Louise, isn't that sweet, how lovely. How many did you make of them, 50 or so?' And I said,

'No, I made 5,000.' And he said, 'What? You're crazy! You'll never sell 5,000 of these!'

"Now the reason I did 5,000 was because I discovered from the church printer that the more you made, the less they charged per piece to print them. So I had 5,000 printed, and they cost 25 cents apiece. I charged a dollar. I never did it to make money, though—I simply wanted to share information. But eventually I *did* sell all 5,000."

So the fact that Dr. Barker thought you were crazy didn't deter you?

"No. I kept moving forward. Once I had the little blue book in hand, I sent a free copy with an order form to every metaphysical church I could find, and several of them bought more. And then a few people ordered it here and there. It grew very slowly. The first year I made $42. I was so proud of myself that I had a book! To me, it was something that came out of nowhere. I didn't know I could do this, and in two years I had sold 5,000 of them. That was when I revamped it.

"I used to go to the church bookstore and watch people. I noticed that if someone picked up my book, they usually bought it. But most people didn't pick it up, so I realized it needed a better title. I renamed it *Heal Your Body* and expanded the material. By that time people were sending me letters with questions about their health and their lives, and I would sit in front of an early version of a word processor and think about what they wrote, and my fingers would start typing. I found that every time I replied to a letter, I'd get a reply back saying, 'How did you know?! How did you know?!' and that gave me more confidence in what I was saying. Eventually I left the church and developed my own process of working with people."

How did your counseling work change once you left the church?

"I used to do what I called short-term therapy—five or six sessions—because either you got what I was talking about and your life was changing or you didn't and there was no point in wasting your money or my time. Some people didn't get it—they'd come once or twice and think the whole thing was stupid. But if you *could* get it or at least work with it, you would see your life change for the better.

"We'd have our session, and toward the end I'd have them lie down while I put some soft music on—I used Steven Halpern's because I didn't get bored with it and it was very peaceful. I'd then have the client close their eyes and do some deep breathing while I invited them to relax their body from either the head down or the feet up. Finally, I would do a treatment for the person. I would put it on tape and then let them go home with it. If they came again, I always had them bring the tape so I could add to it. Eventually people would have a tape filled with positive messages that I wanted them to listen to every night when they went to sleep to reinforce the treatment. Each of them knew that the moment they stopped to listen, they could relax and have only positive things being said to them."

So you were developing your own way of working with clients, and you published your first little book. What happened next?

"Well, it was right around this time when I was diagnosed with cancer. Of course, it scared the hell out of me like it does for anyone. You become terrified when you get that diagnosis. And I remember calling my teacher, crying, 'Eric! Eric! They say that I have cancer!' And he said, 'Louise, you cannot have done all this work on yourself to die of cancer. Let's take a positive approach.' And that immediately calmed me down. He was someone I trusted and believed in, and I knew he was on my side. Therein began my healing."

But as you worked with individuals, I imagine you must have heard stories from people who felt better or were healing themselves with your guidance. Didn't that give you some peace of mind that you could deal with this?

"Yes, well, it was one thing to see the positive changes in other people's lives, but another to believe it for myself now that I was faced with my own life-threatening diagnosis. I realized that Life was giving me a chance to prove to myself that what I was teaching really worked."

So you received the cancer diagnosis and began practicing on yourself?

"It was marvelous, really, because everything I needed came my way as soon as I became determined to heal myself. I found a nutritionist who wasn't going to treat me at first because you weren't supposed to be able to treat cancer with anything but chemotherapy. He was leery of offering me a different approach. I remember he told me to go out into the waiting room and sit a little while. He saw a couple of other patients and then had me come back in. We started talking, and he discovered that I was a member of the Church of Religious Science. Turns out he was with the church, too, and suddenly everything changed. He took me on as a patient, and I learned a tremendous amount about nutrition, which I knew nothing of at the time. My diet was not very good back then.

"After finding the nutritionist, I then found a good therapist and delved into much of the childhood stuff that needed to be healed. I did a lot of screaming and beating pillows to get my anger out. I also learned that forgiveness had a lot to do with healing, and I had to practice forgiveness. I had some cleaning up to do."

I'd like to talk about forgiveness for a minute, I interject. I know you had a violent past, and I'm wondering if the emotional detox work you were doing with the therapist happened *before* the forgiveness process began. I ask this because I've often found that people rush to forgive in the hopes of avoiding the painful feelings that come up when dealing with betrayal, loss, or abuse of any kind.

"Yes, I needed to heal first," Louise replies. "What I realized, and focused on a lot, was the fact that my parents were born beautiful little babies. I needed to look at how they got from this place of innocence to where they were mishandling me. I pieced together as much as I could of their stories—the stories that had been told, anyway—and I realized that my parents had been brought up under terrible circumstances. If you go into the backgrounds of some of the most horrendous people in the world, you always find a terrible, terrible childhood. Some people like me end up wanting to help others, and some want to get even. But you can never get even. I was able to forgive my parents because I understood their lives."

So, to heal yourself from cancer, you enlisted the help of a good nutritionist and a therapist, and you practiced forgiveness. What else?

"Once I put myself in a position where I knew I could be healed, it seemed that everything I needed came to me. Silly little things happened. For example, I heard that foot reflexology was a powerful way to help cleanse the body of toxins. One evening while attending a lecture, I decided to sit in the back row even though I always sat in the front. It wasn't two minutes later when this man came and sat beside me, and he turned out to be a foot reflexologist. When I found out that he went to people's homes, I knew I was meant to meet him. So I had him come to me three times a week. It was part of what I needed. I remember when he first worked on my feet, they felt like glass as he worked to remove those toxins."

So your healing involved a holistic process of working with the body, the mind and its thoughts, and the emotions?

"Yes. Six months later I went back to the doctor, and the cancer was gone. Gone. At that point, my inner ding—my intuition—was telling me it was gone, but I still wanted medical confirmation. Once I had it, I felt that anything could be healed if you're willing to do the work."

I appreciated Louise's acknowledgment that the healing of her cancer was a holistic process—a process that involved her mind, body, *and* emotions . . . not simply relying on "thinking good thoughts" to make the cancer go away.

"No, it's everything," she says. "If you put yourself in a position where you know you can be healed, the right help will come to you. Then you have to be willing to do the work."

What does it take to put yourself in a position to attract what you need to heal?

"You first need to change your thinking about the problem. We all have ideas about healing and how things should and shouldn't work. We need to shift our thinking from *It can't be done* to *It <u>can</u> be done—I just have to figure out how.* I've always said that the word *incurable* means that it can't be cured by any *outer* means at the moment, so we need to go within. That, of course, would mean changing your thinking. You also need to develop self-worth—you need to believe that you are worthy of being healed. If you can develop that as a strong belief and affirmation, then Life will bring you what you need to manifest the healing."

So, if someone were reading this right now and dealing with their own health crisis, what kind of affirmations might you suggest to get them in the right state of mind?

"I'd start with these:

I love myself, and I forgive myself.

I forgive myself for allowing my [anger, fear, resentment, or what have you] *to harm my body.*

I deserve to be healed.

I am worthy of being healed.

My body knows how to heal itself.

I cooperate with my body's nutritional needs.

I feed my body delicious, healthy foods.

I love every inch of my body.

I see cool, clear water flowing through my body and washing away all impurities.

My healthy cells grow stronger every day.

I trust Life to support my healing in every way.

Every hand that touches my body is a healing hand.

My doctors are amazed by how quickly my body is healing.

Every day in every way I am growing healthier and healthier.

I love myself.

I am safe.

Life loves me.

I am healed and whole."

So, while you were healing from cancer, did you continue to see people?

"Yes, and I didn't tell anyone about my diagnosis except my teacher and the people who directly supported me. I didn't want to be influenced by other people's fear. I didn't want to be sidetracked. Once I received notice that the cancer was gone, I began to reevaluate my life, and I made a decision to leave New York. I had been there 30 years, and I was fed up with the weather and the winters. I wanted to go back to where I could have sunshine and flowers all year, so I came to California."

And you settled in Los Angeles?

"That's right. For the first six months I went to the beach a lot. I had a sense that soon I was going to be really busy and wouldn't have time to get to the beach. I also took *Heal Your Body* to every metaphysical meeting I could find in Los Angeles, and if it was appropriate, I'd give someone a copy of it. It turned out that none of the meetings were anything I wanted to go to a second time. They didn't have anything for me. I was putting little feelers out, though, and gradually I started to attract a few clients."

So in some way you were starting all over again. Did you keep in touch with your clients from New York?

"Yes, I stayed in touch with them by phone as I built a new life for myself in Los Angeles.

"There was this marvelous bookstore in West Hollywood called the Bodhi Tree—I took my book to them a couple of times, but they weren't interested. But pretty soon Life began sending people into the store, saying, 'I want that little blue book.' Half the people didn't know the title or my name, but they knew enough to ask for the little blue book. The store finally made the connection that it was me and called to order six copies. As soon as I hung up, I got in the car and zipped down there to hand-deliver them. For the first year, every time I got an order, I would hand-deliver it to the bookstore, and I discovered they were selling more and more. This was also how people learned of me and my work and started to seek my help.

"As I began working with individual clients more, I also started to offer small classes, usually for about six people. Little lectures and classes that people discovered through word of mouth. Over time my audiences expanded, and I got to the point where 350 people would show up to attend the workshops. I believed in what I was teaching, and those who attended were making big changes and getting good results. I then thought that if I could put this experience down on paper—what I was learning from my work—I could help so many more people. But I didn't have the time. Then a woman who had been a client of mine in New York came to see me, and she gave me $2,000 because she was so pleased with the work I had done to help her change her life. I decided this was it!

"I gave myself six months to write the book. I gathered information from my clients, my workshops, and the stories I heard, and began putting it all into the book, along with the content from *Heal Your Body*. That's how *You Can Heal Your Life* got started. I remember once it was published, I would put a stack of books out on a table at a workshop, put change in a bowl, and people would come up and make a purchase by themselves. I had very little money then so I couldn't print a lot of books, but as soon as the ones I did print sold, I went and printed more."

So it was the completion of the first edition of *You Can Heal Your Life* and your successful work with clients that expanded your reach and the size of your audiences?

"Yes, and the word spread far beyond where I was teaching. At some point I went to Australia all by myself—somebody had invited me to do a free lecture on a Friday evening and then a weekend workshop. When I arrived at the venue on Friday evening, there were a thousand people, and I thought, *Where the hell did these people come from?! What are they doing here? How can they know me?* Life sort of took this whole thing over."

Buoyed by her growing trust in how she was being guided by Life, Louise's work and exposure would rise to a whole new level when the AIDS epidemic hit in the mid-'80s.

As she explains now, "There were a few gay men in my practice, and one day someone called me up and asked, 'Louise, would you be willing to start a group for people with AIDS?' I wasn't sure what I would do, but I said, 'Yes, let's get together and see what happens.' So we started with six people, and the next day a man called back and said that this was the first time he'd slept in three months. Then the word got out quickly.

"I didn't know what I was doing, but at that time I knew that no one else knew what they were doing either. It wasn't as though there were brilliant people doing great things for people with AIDS and along came silly me. We were all on the same page. I decided that I was just going to do what I've always done: focus on releasing resentment, help people love themselves, and encourage them to practice forgiveness—the simple things in life.

"With this particular group, I knew that we were dealing with a lot of self-hatred, more so than most people, along with all the judgments society had against them. The gay population had all the stuff that everybody else has with their parents, in addition to often being disowned by them. And then, of course, they were being called an abomination to God. How the hell are you going to have any self-esteem when you keep hearing stuff like *that?* It's impossible. So here I was, this wounded child who had been abandoned by her own parents, helping these men who had been abandoned as well. I understood them. I understood where they came from."

It would seem that Life brought them all together in no small part because of Louise's depth of compassion and understanding. What a gift to these men!

"Well, all hell broke loose in 1987 when I was on *The Oprah Winfrey Show* and *The Phil Donahue Show* in the same week," she tells me. "Both shows heard about what I was doing with AIDS, and they wanted me to talk about it. I took five of the guys who were doing well, and we did the *Oprah* show first. She was wonderful. She let us get our message out—that we were treating the whole subject with love, we weren't afraid of each other, and our focus was on loving ourselves.

"I always wanted to keep the focus on the positive. The first thing I said when I started working with these men was, 'We're not going to sit here and play *Ain't it awful.*' We already knew it was awful, and they could go anywhere to play that game. But when you came to my place, we were going to take a positive approach. Anybody who had any news that was positive, or a technique that was positive, could share it."

So people knew they could count on support, empathy, and some kind of good experience?

"Yes, everybody got to share, and there was no judgment. And the longer we held the meetings, the more goodies I had for them. I remember when someone gave us six massage tables. The men would schlep them to the venue every Wednesday night and we'd set them up. We asked anyone who did Reiki or massage work to stand by a table so people could receive an energy treatment. We didn't call them 'healing tables,' we called them 'energy tables.' For a lot of guys it was the only time someone touched them all week long. That meant a lot to these men. Our focus was simple: feeling good. My ideas have always been simple. It seems the simpler you are, the better things work.

"Being on *Oprah* and *Phil Donahue* in the same week really put us on the map. The few phones we had were constantly jammed, and *You Can Heal Your Life* spent 13 weeks on the *New York Times* bestsellers list. Suddenly I had a company."

So *that* was the point you realized that you actually had a business?

"I never said I wanted to have a business, but I remember saying to myself many years earlier that if I ever did, I would call it Hay House. So there I was. First I had the little blue book, then *You Can Heal Your Life,* and then two meditation tapes—one for the morning and one for the evening. I had four products. I did everything I could by myself at first, but when it got to be too much, I hired someone to help me. Then when things got even busier, I hired someone else; and the business grew very, very slowly from there. It started as a little Hay House. Soon I had five or six people working with me, and I remember giving them each $50 one Christmas because that's all I had to share.

"I was running the business out of my home in an apartment building, and at one point a couple of neighbors complained, so I had to move. I went to another building, which wasn't too far away, and noticed that there was an accounting firm across the hall. We were at a point where we needed a decent accountant, so I hired the firm to help us get our financial records and taxes in order. Eventually, we realized it would cost less to bring someone in full-time, so we ended up hiring one of their employees. Once again, though, Life brought me exactly what I needed to grow and help more people. Before I left for a trip, I thought we had agreed to hire a man named Michael. But when I returned, I discovered that Reid Tracy had been hired instead. Reid is now the president and CEO of Hay House. He ended up being the perfect man for the job."

I'm noticing a theme, I say to Louise. You consistently talk about things growing slowly.

"Yes. Today so many people want fast success. But when we're on the spiritual path and responding to what Life presents us, I think the most powerful work we do happens gradually over time. It's almost as though we don't realize it's happening. We look back and think, *Oh my, look at all that!*"

In addition to measured and steady success, I was noticing other key, recurring themes while listening to Louise's spiritual journey:

- *Simplicity*—focusing on small, simple, and manageable steps instead of making things complicated.

- *Optimism*—putting attention and energy toward solutions rather than focusing on problems.
- *Patience*—experiencing the journey fully and consciously rather than rushing to achieve a particular result.
- *Trust*—learning to trust Life by seeing the perfection and opportunity for growth in all our experiences.
- *Growth*—viewing life as a classroom where we use our experiences as catalysts for change and self-realization.
- *Service*—focusing more on how we can best encourage and assist those in need, as opposed to getting lost in our own personal vision and quest for success.
- *Action*—making a commitment to show up and walk through the doors that Life opens for us on our journey.
- *Faith*—being willing to take chances and keep moving forward without knowing the outcome.

- *Magnetism*—developing and tapping into the ability to attract what we need by putting (and keeping) ourselves in the right state of mind.

I have one final question for Louise before we wrap up our first meeting: *Do you think Life is continually tapping us on the shoulder, and if we just pay attention and do what's before us, we're likely to find the right path?*

"I think that will keep you busy," she replies. "There are a lot of people who need goals in life—a one-year goal or a five-year goal—but that was never me. I wasn't really trying to do anything that was well defined or narrowly focused. My question was always: *How can I help people?* I have asked that question thousands of times, and I continue to ask it today. When I see all the difficult things that are happening in the world, I realize that I might not be able to do anything specific, but what I *can* do is ask the question and project the intention energetically of *How might I help?*

"Once we understand how this works, and trust how it works, we simply answer the phone and open the mail."

CHAPTER TWO

BECOMING THE CREATOR OF AN EXCEPTIONAL LIFE

"We are powerful, creative beings who determine our future with every thought we think and every word we speak." This is the first thing Louise says when I turn on the voice recorder at the start of our next session.

We're sitting opposite each other, stretched out on a long window seat in my hotel room, overlooking the city of Toronto below. It's a beautiful, sunny afternoon. As I consider Louise's remark, I realize that, at its core, this message is one of the most important: *In our purest, most positive state of mind, we are powerful creators of our very best lives.* When we think good thoughts, we feel good. When we feel good, we make good choices. When we feel good and make good choices, we draw more good experiences into our lives. It really *is* that simple . . . and elegant . . . and true.

Science tells us that energy waves are the "stuff" of the Universe, and that every breath we take and every thought we think has a direct effect on something or someone in it. The chair I sit on, the keyboard I use to write, and the beautiful magnolia tree outside my window are all made of energy. The speed with which an object vibrates determines the density of the form. This energy is directly influenced by the thoughts we think, the words we speak, and the actions we take. *These thoughts, words, and actions produce feelings; and our feelings become the currency with which we purchase our life experiences.*

As Louise and I talk about the ways in which our thoughts influence our lives, I become even more aware of how significant and powerful this idea really is. So much of what we both believe, teach, and practice in our own lives is based on a concept that is still seen by many as far-fetched, New Age, or simplistic at best.

For a moment, I imagine myself searching the web, my personal library, or the minds of my colleagues in the scientific community for solid evidence to back up our ideas. But then I remember, I don't do that anymore. I no longer defend the spiritual principles that have guided and shaped my life. They work and I know it. Louise and I both know it.

As we continue our conversation that afternoon, it becomes clear that Louise and I have each been inspired by New Thought writers such as Emmet Fox and Florence Scovel Shinn, who encouraged readers to use the power of thought to change and improve their lives. By applying these principles to our own lives, Louise and I have been able to manifest opportunities and experiences that we believe are proof of how powerful our thoughts can be. And this evidence has reinforced our beliefs.

While science may ignore anecdotal evidence from people who experience the healing or creative power of thought, the stories are important. They are harbingers of change, catalysts for a shift in consciousness that will ultimately shape the way we live. Miraculous stories and extraordinary experiences often precede understanding. They invite us to open our hearts and minds, making it possible to believe in something that exists *outside* of our limited thinking. And that's the point.

Evolutionary leaps of consciousness often begin with ideas that seem magical or astounding. Just think about how crazy the idea of seeing images on a box in their living room must have sounded to people when they first heard about "television." One wild, seemingly impossible idea changed the face of humanity forever.

As a pioneer in the mind-body field, Louise has challenged her readers and audiences to expand their thinking by suggesting that they treat physical ailments with metaphysical tools. Rather than focus on treating disease with conventional methods alone, she invited people to also focus on how they *thought* about their illness. By making the link between the mind and the body, she allowed others to discover what she herself experienced: that our thoughts do indeed play an integral role in the healing of the body. Louise has seen the evidence of this repeatedly in the smiling faces of men and women who have healed their bodies and their lives. That's enough proof for her and the many people she's helped on the healing path.

When it comes to harnessing the power of thought, we simply need to act in new ways and trust that Life will present us with our own proof. So with this in mind, I surrender my quest to prove that thought influences physical reality, and instead rely upon my own real-life anecdotal evidence. Once I make this decision, something interesting happens.

While grocery shopping with my husband, Michael, later that evening, I stopped at the flower department to look at some orchids. I stood there for quite some time studying them, taking in their vibrant colors and the exquisite shape of their petals. As I examined each one, I considered buying one, but changed my mind after being distracted by a question from a nearby shopper.

The next day I returned home from a meeting to find a large box sitting on my front steps. I dragged it inside, opened it up, and discovered an exquisite white orchid nestled inside the box. I instantly recalled my intention the night before and saw this gift as the result of focused, positive thought. I adore flowers, and I've had enough experiences like this to know that if I direct my energy—even in a small way—toward them, it sends a powerful signal to the Universe that I believe actually draws them to me. This time, the signal must have been even stronger than usual. Two days later, I received an unexpected delivery from a friend on the West Coast . . . another beautiful white orchid.

What we put out into the world has a great effect on what we get back. Most of us are shown examples of this every day, but we never make the connection. "We are constantly working in cooperation with Life," Louise reminds me, "and we want to inspire people to practice so they, too, can experience the evidence in their own lives. We simply need to keep an open mind and trust our own experience." I couldn't agree more. At any given moment, we see, feel, send, and affect energy in ways we seldom, if ever, imagine.

Have you ever walked into a room and instantly known that someone nearby was angry? Or looked into the eyes of a stranger and felt overwhelmed by a feeling of compassion, understanding, or love? This is what happens when we *receive* energy. We tune in to our environment, pick up on the vibe, and download information about what's going on, often without the need for discussion or explanation.

Of course, we also *send* energy. Have you ever been afraid of getting sick and wondered if worrying about it had anything to do with it actually happening? Or have you ever desired something so intensely that it seemed as though your focus on the object of desire had something to do with it miraculously showing up in your life? These are the things that can happen when we *transmit* energy. By sending out signals in the form of thoughts, words, or actions, we energetically influence our environment—and, subsequently, our life experiences.

Years ago I was fortunate enough to have an extraordinary chance to experience the power of transmitting energy.

After a busy year of traveling and speaking, I was feeling tired and creatively blocked. During this time I was scheduled to visit Miraval Resort & Spa in Tucson, Arizona, for a business meeting. Before heading there, I contacted my friend and colleague Wyatt Webb, the author of *It's Not about the Horse*.

Wyatt created the Equine Experience at Miraval—a process that uses interactions with horses as a mirror for how human beings relate to each other and the world. I trusted Wyatt and knew he was an insightful, experienced guide who could help me understand why I was blocked and how to move past it.

On our way to the stables, Wyatt and I caught each other up on our lives. When we arrived at the round horse pen, I recognized an old friend. Standing by a fence under the shade of a few trees was Monsoon.

Monsoon is 17 hands high and weighs more than 1,200 pounds—and although I knew this magnificent creature from previous visits to Miraval, I felt myself get anxious as Wyatt directed me toward him. I stepped into the pen, curious to know what he might teach me.

Wyatt and I talked for a while about how I was feeling and the changes that had occurred in my life over the last couple of years. After listening to me and watching my body for clues (Wyatt is masterful at discovering what's going on inside a person by observing what's going on outside), he announced, "You know what's happening, Cheryl? I think you're really, really pissed off, and this unexpressed anger is blocking your energy."

As I listened to his words, I did my best to raise a wall of protection between my friend and my increasingly raw emotions. I took a step back and looked away. But I knew I needed help, and I trusted him enough to let my feelings out, so I allowed myself to let the tears flow.

Wyatt stood by my side, a silent witness to my pain and frustration. When I stopped crying, he gently explained that my anger held the key to my power—and if I didn't allow myself to feel it, I would never be able to fully own and express my true potential during the next stage of my life.

"You've got a lot of power inside that body of yours," he told me, "and unless you're willing to move through the anger to connect with the energy on the 'underside,' you'll keep feeling stuck."

To this day, what happened next still amazes me.

Wyatt led me to Monsoon, who was standing against a fence sniffing the ground below him. His head was positioned away from us, his body parallel to the fence. When we were about 20 feet from the horse's hindquarters, Wyatt said, "I want you to use your energy to move that horse. I want Monsoon to turn completely around so his head is facing us."

"You want me to move the horse with my mind?"

"No," Wyatt replied. "I want you to move the horse with your energy. Close your eyes, take several deep breaths, and tell that horse to *move!*"

I stood very still, closed my eyes, and focused as hard as I could on moving the horse. In my mind I kept screaming, *MOVE! MOVE! MOVE!* But he didn't budge.

Wyatt came closer to me. And in his direct yet soft-spoken cowboy drawl, he said, "Stop using your head, Cheryl. Use your *gut*." He poked me gently in the stomach. "Move the horse from *here*."

I closed my eyes again, determined to take my time. With each deep breath, I imagined myself creating a growing mass of intense energy deep in my abdomen. Then, when I was ready, I imagined moving this energy out of my body toward Monsoon while holding the intention that he *move*. After a few moments, he lifted his head, looked back at us, and proceeded to walk in a complete circle. That horse was now facing me, gazing directly into my eyes.

I stood there dumbfounded, staring at Monsoon. Then I turned back to Wyatt, who looked me right in the eye and said, "Now, just imagine what that kind of power can do for you and others in the world."

I've never forgotten that moment or that message.

We are all exquisite communication machines. Each one of us is a walking, talking radio tower, transmitting and receiving energy signals every moment of every day. Like radiant stars sparkling in the night sky, we live and breathe in a unified field of energy that connects us to one another. Every movement or casual or random thought goes out into this field and affects it in some way.

As we learn to pay closer attention to the signals we receive and send out, we claim ownership of a vast creative power that not only affects us, but everyone and everything around us. With practice, we can become more confident in our ability to use this energetic network to make life better by tuning our transmitter—our thoughts—to a more positive frequency.

Back in my hotel room in Toronto, Louise shares a story that illustrates this point beautifully. "I was driving to the office thinking about an upsetting letter I received earlier in the day," she says. "I was ruminating about it, having an argument with the person who wrote it in my head. But then I caught myself. I stopped and realized that this way of thinking wasn't making me feel good. So I pulled over and started telling myself what I needed to hear to feel better. I said things like:

I release this incident with love; it is over and done.

I look with expectation to my next moment,
which is fresh and new.

Only good experiences lie before me.

I am greeted with love wherever I go.

I love Life, and Life loves me.

All is well, and so am I.

"In no time I was back on a positive track and was on my way. A moment later, I switched on the radio and was greeted by a sweeping, inspirational piece of classical music that made me smile from ear to ear. I knew a shift had occurred. I arrived at the office feeling so much better. When I walked through the front door, an employee greeted me with 'I love you.' When I got to my desk, there was a vase of flowers waiting for me—a gift from the spouse of an employee. And I discovered that a problem I needed to discuss with someone at a meeting later that day had been completely resolved and I didn't need to attend the meeting after all. It was at that moment I said out loud, 'Thank you. Thank you. Thank you.'"

As I listen to Louise share this story, I jot down the first instruction she gave herself: "I started telling myself what I needed to hear to feel better." What a beautiful example of how *our first, most important act of self-care is caring for our thoughts.* When we do so, everyone benefits.

By catching herself quickly and turning things around with loving inner dialogue, Louise sent out an energetic message to Life, which responded in a way that not only uplifted her, but also enriched the experiences of those around her.

I'll say it again: your thoughts directly influence your life. It's easy to get caught up in a debate about how this principle works, whether or not it works, or the validity of thought creating reality. But debating these ideas is like expending precious energy arguing about how a radio works rather than simply turning on the station to enjoy your favorite program, or questioning the legitimacy of the Internet instead of using it to communicate or gain information. At this point in time, using spiritual rather than intellectual tools requires faith and an open mind. Spiritual tools make life easier and more rewarding.

"I was once in a class with Virginia Satir, the internationally known pioneer of family therapy," Louise tells me, "and she talked about having done a study with students on different ways to wash dishes. By gathering their answers, she came up with 250 *different* ways to do dishes, and every person thought theirs was the only way to do it right. When you close your mind to new ideas or new ways of doing things, you might miss out on easier, better ways.

"Cheryl, you and I are trying to connect people with an easier way to live an exceptional life. When they understand the concept and put it into practice—by thinking thoughts and making choices that make them feel good—they'll put themselves in a state of flow with the Universe, and miracles will start to happen. Then they'll get all the evidence they need. Things they couldn't even imagine will begin to occur."

You are an extraordinary spiritual machine. Right now, there are more than 50 trillion cells in your body, all working together, enabling you to read this sentence. Your cells don't argue. They don't question how things work. And they don't engage in a debate about who's smarter or more efficient. They align together in beautiful harmony to allow the machine called "your body" to function at its highest possible level at any given moment. What a miracle!

This same kind of harmonious interplay takes place in our outer world, too. Every day our creative currency of thoughts, words, actions, and feelings are working in Divine cooperation with the energy of the Universe to create our lives. By focusing our energy in a positive way, we are far more likely to generate good experiences. It's really that simple.

Staking claim to this creative power and using your energy wisely can be challenging at first. After all, most of us have been trained to live in fear and to think and act defensively—looking for what doesn't work, what might go wrong, or what isn't good about our lives. You need only watch a few minutes of the news, or read the headlines of a newspaper or website, to see where the collective focus lies. "Discover the Danger Lurking in Your Drinking Water," "The Economy Takes Another Dive," "Ten Reasons to Keep Your Kids in Full View" . . . these nonstop, fear-inducing messages can affect you in ways you're not even aware of. And, over time, you may actually find yourself drawn to negative news stories, conversations filled with useless drama, and repetitive harmful thoughts. Once this cycle starts, it doesn't stop by itself. You have to be vigilant about making good choices and thinking good thoughts, substituting good for bad at every turn on every road.

Immersing yourself in this fearful, depressing energy perpetuates negativity. For example, you might become obsessed with the latest reality program that shows people at their worst, and begin to find yourself surrounded by individuals who are always in some kind of crisis. Or you may get pulled into drama at work, and begin contributing to the problem by gossiping or complaining about what isn't working in your own life.

Without realizing it, we develop patterns of thought and behavior that direct our radio transmitter to search for *and* emit negative signals that only create more negativity and difficult experiences in our lives. And these patterns can become deeply personal. Every day we can end up stuck in a negative loop, constantly labeling ourselves as defective, bad, or unworthy.

As Louise explains to me now, "When you hate yourself, say mean things to yourself, tell yourself how ugly you are, or hide from a mirror, you start to feel really uncomfortable. You don't feel good at all. You won't enjoy anything in your day, and very little good will come to you. But when you do something as simple as look in the mirror and tell yourself that you love yourself, even when it's hard to do or you don't believe it, your energy shifts. Then, as you go through your day, you feel better and attract better circumstances. That's when silly things happen like getting a parking space when there usually are none to be found, or encountering green lights at every turn."

I wonder about where it all begins. How have we become so out of touch with this power to shape our lives? I ask Louise.

"As children, we are brought up from day one responding to the words *stop* or *no,*" she replies. "They're some of the first words we hear. It has become normal—although it's not natural—for us to be more focused on what we can't do, what we're not allowed to do, and the limiting beliefs that hold us back rather than on our true, magnificent potential. There are lots and lots of people in this world who start every conversation with something negative. It's become normal for them. They walk in the door, for example, and greet you with, 'Oh my goodness, I almost tripped on these stairs.' After a while, it becomes second nature. They don't even know they're doing it. I see examples of this everywhere.

"I was in a store a couple of weeks ago shopping for clothes. I found a few items I wanted to purchase, and as I was ready to pay for them, I overheard three women—one in the dressing room, another standing outside the dressing room, and the woman who was waiting on me—talking to one another. Soon enough, the conversation turned to some negative experience that had occurred, which inspired them to start topping each other. I took my card and said, 'I'll be back. I can't deal with this negativity right now.' So I left and came back much later. I asked the girl behind the counter, 'Is that conversation over now?' She laughed as I finished my purchase. People are drawn to positive experiences. These women had no idea that their negative conversation was driving a customer out of the store—and I'm sure there could have been others who walked out without ever saying a word."

So we'll continue our journey with an emphasis on the positive? I ask with a smile.

"You know, there are so many wonderful teachers—Dr. Wayne Dyer, Abraham, Dr. Christiane Northrup—who all share the same message," Louise tells me. "I think the real goal in life is to feel good. We want money because we want to feel better. We want good health because we want to feel better. We want a nice relationship because we think we will feel better. And if we could just make feeling better our goal, we would eliminate a lot of extra work. How can I really feel good in this moment? What thoughts can I think *right now* that will make me feel better? That's the question we need to constantly be asking ourselves."

As I turn off the recorder and gather my things, I think to myself, *Amen, sister.*

CHAPTER THREE

How You Start Your Day Is How You Live Your Day

I've spent the morning walking around Covent Garden in London. It's an early fall day, and the street performers and artisans are setting up shop preparing for the crowds. I adore London. I love the diversity; the kind and gracious people; and the scrumptious variety of fashion, food, shops, and cafés.

Louise and I are here for an event, and we're scheduled to meet in the afternoon to continue our work on this book. I'm so looking forward to it. In the short amount of time we've been meeting, my life has already been affected in such a positive way. I'm more mindful of my thoughts throughout the day, for instance. And the time it takes for me to catch myself when I start ruminating about something unpleasant is getting shorter and shorter. I'm also weighing my choices, both personal and professional, to see whether or not I feel good once a decision is made. If it doesn't feel good, *no* is becoming an automatic response. How wonderful to be growing and learning while writing a book. . . .

When I knock on Louise's hotel-room door, she greets me with her sparkling blue eyes and a big smile. I feel instantly welcomed. We chat about the morning and then get down to business. I nestle into a spot on the floor in front of the coffee table, tap on the recorder, and begin our session by asking Louise what's on her mind.

"We must teach people how to begin their day," she replies with intense determination. "The first hour of the morning is crucial. How you spend it will determine your experience for the rest of your day."

And we're off! Louise's passion is evident, and I laugh out loud as this elegant woman starts the lesson with: "Too many people start their day with 'Oh, shit! It's another day and I've got to get up, damn it!' If you have a lousy way of starting your day, you're not going to have a good day ever—it's not possible. If you do your best to have the morning be awful, your day will be awful."

As I listen to her talk, I'm pulled back to my mid-20s and the intimate relationship I had with the snooze button on my alarm clock. Back then it was a game to see how long I could stay in bed before dragging myself out to go to work. I didn't like my life much, and I certainly didn't look forward to going to my job.

Now, as I sit here with Louise, I think about the millions of men and women who hit the snooze button every day or greet the morning with dread. I wince as I think about the energetic message this sends out into the world: *I don't want to wake up, I hate where I'm going today,* or *I'd rather go back to sleep than get up and face my crummy life.* Thoughts like these just bring people more of the same.

It's a game changer when you realize that how you start your day sets in motion a pattern of thinking that determines your experiences all day long. Curious to know how Louise starts her day, I ask her to share the details.

"I have this little routine I've done for years. The moment I wake up, I snuggle my body a little more into my bed, feel the feeling of the bed, and thank it for a really good night's sleep. I do this for a few minutes as I start my day with positive thoughts. I tell myself things like: *This is a good day. This is going to be a really good day.* Then I get up, use the bathroom, and thank my body for working well. I spend a little time stretching. I have a bar in the doorway of the bathroom that I hang from—I bring my knees up to my chest three times and then hang from it. I find that hanging in the morning is a very good thing."

I imagine Louise hanging from a bar in her bathroom doorway, and in my mind I start walking around my house looking for the perfect place to hang a bar, too. The idea sounds like a lot of fun to me.

"After I do a few stretches, I make a cup of tea and take it back to bed. I love my bed. I've had the headboard specially built at an angle so I can lean up against it when I read or write. I've carried this headboard with me for years. It's an example of something I've done to make my bedroom special and comfortable—a sanctuary. It's a lovely place to be."

What else makes your bedroom special?

"That I'm in it," Louise quickly replies with a wide, childlike grin. As we both laugh, I'm tempted to walk over and pinch the cheek of the little girl I see in those twinkling eyes. But I quickly restrain my own inner kid and allow her to continue.

"When I've gone back to bed, I then do a bit of spiritual reading. I usually have a few things I'm reading at one time." I interrupt for a moment to find out what she's currently enjoying. "Well, I keep my book

Heart Thoughts with me because it's easy to read a few short passages in one sitting. I also have Alan Cohen's *A Deep Breath of Life* nearby. And right now I'm rereading Florence Scovel Shinn's *The Game of Life and How to Play It.* It's a very good book. If there's time after relaxing and reading, I might do a crossword puzzle. I stretch my body and then I stretch my mind. It's a morning ritual. Then I start to get up."

Louise's morning routine sounds like the perfect way to begin the day, and I wonder how much time it takes. "I try to give myself two hours before I face people. I like to be able to do things in a leisurely way," she tells me. "I've learned to take my time. I might sit in bed and think about what I'm going to have for breakfast—something delicious and good for the body, something I will really enjoy.

"If there's an important activity that I'm going to do that day, I make sure to do a lot of positive affirmations around it, and I always do them in the present tense, as if the situation is already occurring. For example, if I have an interview, I tell myself: *I know this is a wonderful interview. It is an easy flow of ideas between myself and the other person. The person is very glad for the information I give them. Everything goes smoothly and effortlessly, and both of us are pleased."*

I'm amazed by Louise's ability to be positive and so upbeat. By now we've spent enough time together for me to see that her disposition is consistent. This woman clearly lives in a positive world of her own making. Because this is so unusual, I can't help but wonder if she ever feels bad. So, as she wraps up the description of her morning ritual, I ask: Do you ever have a bad day, wake up in a bad mood, or feel depressed?

Louise takes her time to carefully consider my question before responding. "Not much anymore," she finally says. "I've been practicing a long time, and I have good habits in place. It's all about practice. . . ."

We decide to take a break, but as we chat, I keep the recorder running just in case. Good thing. We both realize that by inviting people to stop and think about how they behave during routine moments of the day—what they say to themselves as they go through these rituals of living—we're tapping into a valuable process for reprogramming the subconscious mind.

Every day, in little ways, we deepen the groove of habitual thoughts that directly influence the quality of our lives by what we think and say to ourselves on a regular basis. The more we shift our internal monologue to language that serves a better life, the better our lives become. It's the little daily rituals that give us the most chance for change.

"Too many people think you need to go somewhere to quietly focus on affirmations," Louise explains, "but we're doing affirmations all the time. Everything we think and say to ourselves is an affirmation. We need to be conscious of what we're saying and thinking all the time so that life can get better."

She then offers examples of questions we need to consider: "What's the first thing you say to yourself when you wake up in the morning? What do you think about while in the shower? When shaving? What do you say to yourself as you pick out your clothes, get dressed, put on makeup, or dry your hair? What are you saying to your family as you make breakfast or get the children ready for school? These are all moments that can be put to good use."

In the last few years, I've grown to understand the importance of starting the day in a more peaceful and intentional way. After supporting my husband, Michael, through a four-year-long illness, we came out the other side changed people. Both of us gained a new appreciation for gentleness, for being kinder to ourselves and each other. We allowed ourselves to live life with more of a focus on comfort and self-care.

After suffering from the special kind of burnout that occurs when tending to a loved one on a long-term basis, I could no longer pop out of bed like toast from a toaster and plunge headfirst into my day. For too many years I was in a perpetual battle with my to-do list, desperately racing to get things done so I could finally relax and enjoy my life. Now I relax and enjoy my life *first.*

Listening to Louise describe the start of her day fills me with ideas about how to build upon the changes I've already made to my mornings since Michael's illness. At the moment, my day starts once I'm downstairs making a cup of tea. I take it into our sunroom with my journal and favorite pen. I've kept a diary since the age of 12, and writing has grown to be an important act of emotional and creative self-care. I write about whatever comes to mind before finishing up with a page of positive affirmations. This is my way of pointing my thoughts in the right direction for the day. Then I might watch an inspiring video or read a bit from a favorite book or website.

My tastes are eclectic—I love everything from biographies or spiritual and inspirational books to human-interest stories and the latest news about health, science, and technology. I also love funny videos! This time has become vital to my well-being;

these are moments when I can be reinspired, replenished, and fed on a soul level.

Like Louise, I've done my best to avoid appointments, meetings, or conversations in the morning. I want time to myself where I'm able to stay connected to my own thoughts and feelings. I've started scheduling appointments, office work, phone calls, and the like after noontime so my mornings are free for writing and other creative projects. While I might decide to work earlier, I want to know that I have the space and the silence to stay focused on my top priorities.

I recognize that to most people, it's a luxury to be able to spend time in the morning in this way. In the past, whenever I was going a hundred miles an hour (or when I was employed by someone else and needed to get to work), I was lucky to have ten minutes to myself. But even ten minutes can make a difference.

Louise agrees. "We need to start somewhere. If you are a busy mom or dad who needs to get the children ready for school, or if you have to get to work early, it's still important to give yourself some time to start your day off in the right way. I would rather wake up earlier to have this extra time in the morning. Even if you only give yourself 10 or 15 minutes, that's good—it's your time for self-care. This is absolutely necessary.

"I haven't always had the time I do now," she continues. "We begin with small steps. When you get up, it's important to do a ritual that feels good to you, to say something to yourself that makes you feel good. *Life loves me* is a good start. It's a very comfortable thing to say. Then, make sure what you eat for breakfast is comforting—something delicious and good for you. Nourish your body with a good morning meal; and nourish your mind with good, comforting thoughts."

Right out of bed, we can all use the power of affirmations to set up the day in the best possible way. Here are a few examples of what you can say to yourself as you go through your morning:

When you first wake up and open your eyes:

Good morning, bed, thank you for being so comfortable. I love you.

Darling [your name], *this is a blessed day.*

All is well. I have time for everything I need to do today.

Looking in the bathroom mirror:

Good morning, [your name]. *I love you. I really, really love you.*

There are great experiences coming our way today.

You look wonderful.

You have the best smile.

Your makeup [or hair] *looks perfect.*

You are my ideal woman [or man].

We are having a terrific day today.

I love you dearly.

In the shower:

I love my body, and my body loves me.

It is such a pleasure to take a shower.

The water feels so good.

I am grateful for the people who designed and built this shower.

My life is so blessed.

Using the bathroom:

I easily release all that my body no longer needs.

Intake, assimilation, and elimination are all in Divine right order.

Getting dressed:

I love my closet.

It is so easy for me to get dressed.

I always pick the best thing to wear.

I am comfortable in my clothing.

I trust my inner wisdom to pick the perfect outfit for me.

Louise notes that starting the day off right can also be fun and extremely important when you have children. "The morning is often a time of push-pull between parents and children. If we can get in the habit of doing positive affirmations with kids as they're getting dressed or as we're making breakfast, we not only set the whole family up for a good day, we teach children a valuable life skill, too."

I'm immediately reminded of my friend Nancy, who had transformed mornings for her sister's family with a simple game. As Nancy was making a deal with her five-year-old nephew to see if he could stop sucking his thumb until her next visit, her niece decided that she wanted in on the action, too.

Nancy's niece hated mornings and resisted getting up for school. "Isabel was cranky and irritable when woken up," my friend told me, "and her stubbornness created a tremendous amount of stress for the whole family. I asked her what it would take to become a happy morning girl, and she said, 'Seventy-seven dollars.' So I took advantage of the moment and disguised a new positive ritual as a game and agreed to the deal."

Nancy said that she'd give her niece $77 upon her next visit, six weeks later, if she could learn to enjoy mornings. "I told her, 'You're going to have one tap to wake you up in the morning, and then you're going to sit up, greet the day with a smile, and get dressed. You can only sit down for breakfast once you're ready for school.'" Isabel agreed to the game, and the rest was an unexpected success.

"It's been two months, and my sister tells me that this new morning ritual has transformed their lives," Nancy said. "Isabel gets up on time, she's happy, and she's downstairs and ready for breakfast after just one tap. And the funny thing is, she hasn't even asked me for the $77." While this may have started out as a game to make money for Isabel, it's turned into a new daily habit that has transformed the way her entire family starts their day. It seems that a happier family was enough payment for this little girl.

Louise feels strongly about working with kids in this way. "We need to give children ways to help themselves feel good," she tells me. "Parents can start with simple messages throughout the morning that children can repeat—messages such as: *It's so easy to get dressed. I love getting dressed. Breakfast is always a fun time. We're all so glad to see each other. We love eating breakfast together. Breakfast makes my body feel good.*

"Parents can even go around the table and have each family member share one thing they love about themselves. Or they can put affirmations in a bowl and choose one for the whole family to focus on during the day. This can become a morning ritual for couples, families, roommates, and so on. Each person can even decide on one experience they'd like to have that day and create an affirmation for it."

I imagine how different the world would be if we raised children with the skills to manage their thoughts and actions in a positive way. If we invest even one-tenth of the energy we put into schoolwork, sports, or extracurricular activities into developing this critical life skill, we could actually shift consciousness on the planet in a palpable way.

As the time Louise and I spend together in London comes to an end, I notice how excited I am about the prospect of focusing more attention on the start of my day. I tell her I'm committed to being more mindful of my thoughts and actions from the moment I wake up.

"We don't have to make changes all at once," she notes (there's that intuition again—no doubt she hears the overachiever at work!). "Just pick one ritual for the morning and start there. Then, once you have that ritual down, pick another one and keep practicing. Don't overwhelm yourself. Remember, the idea is to feel good."

And feel good I do. As I leave Louise's hotel room, I feel so blessed to be working on this book. Unlike past writing experiences where I felt tortured by deadlines or procrastination, this time I feel inspired and grateful. But how could it be any different? After all, I'm engaged in a master class with a gal who knows how to live well—exceptionally well.

CHAPTER FOUR

How You Live Your Day Is How You Live Your Life

Winter is settling in, normally a time when I feel a bit gloomy and depressed about the fading light and the oncoming cold, snowy weather. But things have changed. I wake up this morning with a smile. As I look out my bedroom window, the sun streams into my eyes, warming my face and neck, and I repeat a ritual started just a few short weeks ago: "Thank you, dear bed, for another wonderful night's rest."

My cat, Poupon, snuggled up next to me in his usual position under my arm, hears my words and stretches his paw up to touch my face. Life is good. For the first time in a long while, I feel excited about winter. I'm looking forward to the fierce beauty of the snowstorms here in the Northeast, the blanket of silence that descends upon our home once the snow has settled, and the chance to hole up and write this book.

Before I get out of bed, I look into Poupon's eyes and say, "Yes, my sweet angel, today is going to be a really, really good day." I'm about to visit Louise at her home in San Diego. A last-minute speaking engagement is giving us the chance to spend a few days working together. I'm off on the next leg of this adventure!

It's such a warm, sunny day in San Diego that it feels like a whole world away from the below-freezing temperatures back home in Massachusetts. I've been traveling for hours, and I'm really looking forward to a cup of tea and a good meal.

The car drops me off in front of a stately building downtown. I step inside the front door, dragging my luggage behind me, and am met by a friendly doorman who takes me to the elevator that will deliver me up to Louise's home.

As the elevator door slowly opens into a small foyer, I'm met by elegant Asian décor and chant music playing softly in the background. I ring the bell, and Louise greets me with that signature smile. "Welcome, darling, come in!"

I cross the threshold into another world. "Is this music always playing?" I ask, looking back at the foyer, intrigued by the idea of welcoming guests with the calming sounds of chanting.

"Yes," she replies quietly, as she closes the door with the gentleness of a monk. She motions for me to follow as I look around in amazement. The place looks and feels like a beautiful spa.

Louise's home is grand; the views are epic; and the décor is bright, cheery, and filled with bold colors. There's a small water fountain softly bubbling in the entryway behind a row of lush, green plants. As I walk by a sweeping staircase, I come face-to-face with a giant statue of Quan Yin—the goddess of compassion. She seems right at home.

The living-room area is wide open, with tall windows that look out over downtown San Diego and Balboa Park. I immediately head toward a striking orchid garden sitting atop a baby grand piano. "Wow, how long have you had this?" I ask. "It's beautiful."

"It was a gift from someone quite a while ago, and I just keep replacing the orchids when necessary."

As I look around the expanse of space, I notice that orchids are a theme. I see them everywhere.

Louise shows me to my room, and we agree to have an early dinner once I've had a chance to unpack and freshen up.

While settling into the guest room, I think about the changes I've made to my morning routine since my last conversation with Louise. Upon returning home from London, I started noticing the habitual thoughts associated with my morning tasks, and I was surprised by what I learned about myself. One thing I discovered, for instance, was a pattern of focusing on problems while taking a shower. No sooner did I start to wash my face or shampoo my hair than my mind would wrap itself around a difficult e-mail I needed to write, a request I wanted to decline, or a looming deadline that had to be met. As my shower progressed, I'd turn the situation over and over in my mind in a futile effort to find a solution so I could feel better. Instead, by the time I was drying off, I'd feel anxious about facing the day.

This practice followed me from the shower to other tasks, such as brushing my teeth, choosing clothes for the day, or getting dressed. The subtle, negative self-talk that accompanied the discovery of a new wrinkle or figure flaw would often expand into bigger conversations in my head about the challenges of aging or the need to lose weight. Clearly I had work to do.

The beauty of awareness is that it interrupts a pattern. Bringing attention to our inner conversations—the things we say to ourselves every single day—is a way of becoming present to the truth. The messages we give ourselves day in and day out deepen a groove in the mind, giving them more power. And they also transmit energy out into the world, drawing back to us the very thing we focus on.

Once I saw how pervasive and entrenched these thought habits were, I went about the business of shifting them. I started affirming the changes I wanted to make, with a focus on self-love and acceptance. I began writing, speaking, and pasting affirmations around my home—little signs that read: *Changing my thoughts is easy and comfortable, I love improving my morning routine,* and *It is a joy to speak to myself in kind and loving ways.* I even put a note in the shower that stated: *I am showered with good thoughts all day long!*

After using many of the affirmations Louise and I had discussed during our last conversation, I noticed changes within just a couple of weeks. These new thoughts were trading places with the old ones, and my mornings were becoming more peaceful and enjoyable. I was programming a far better start to my day, and it felt good . . . *really* good.

Louise and I decide to walk to a neighborhood restaurant for dinner. While we wait for our food, I fill her in on what's been happening at home—my new awareness and the changes I've made in my life since our last visit.

"This is good," she tells me. "You're starting to pay attention. We need to become aware of what we habitually say to ourselves during the day. It's important to start listening. If you notice that you say something more than three times, you're probably saying it a lot. For some people, 'Oh, shit' could be a very repetitive theme. If people get ahold of their day, they get ahold of their life."

I was certainly having that experience myself.

"Let's talk about how to create the day," Louise suggests. "You can start by paying attention to how you leave the house. What do you think or say as you open the door to go out? What do you say as you close the door? What do you say to yourself as you walk down the stairs or when you get in the car? Are you approaching your day with excitement and enthusiasm, or worry and stress? As you leave your home, it's a great time to plan your day, to program what you want to have happen rather than leave it up to chance."

I think about my routines and how I'm certainly not accustomed to programming my day. Instead, I typically walk out the front door and down the steps toward the garage, focused on whether or not

I've turned things off or put away anything my cat might get into while I'm gone. As I get in the car, I go through a mental list of errands and stops I need to make so I can plan a route that will allow me to avoid traffic.

"Let's use driving as an example of one way to start your day differently," Louise proposes. "First of all, have your car be a friend. Talk to it nicely. I often say, 'Hi, darling, how are you, so nice to see you. We're going to have a nice ride to the office.' You might even name your car—I do. And when I leave my home, I affirm: *I am surrounded by good drivers,* and I make sure to send love into all the cars around me. I always like to feel that there's love everywhere on the road."

Louise mentions other affirmations to use when driving, and I quickly jot them down:

My ride is easy and effortless.

My drive goes smoothly, and more
quickly than I expect.

I feel comfortable in the car.

I know this will be a beautiful drive to the office
[or to school, the store, or the like].

I bless my car with love.

I send love to every person on the road.

What a way to travel! As I listen to Louise's driving affirmations, I think about the idea of sending love to every person on the road. Once again, just imagine a world where every driver did that. While it might seem like a crazy idea, I can't help but be inspired by a vision of the future—a world where every human being understands their own spiritual nature and therefore uses the creative power of their mind to fill the world with good intentions. Since thought influences reality, just think about how the planet would change. Maybe the vision isn't so far-fetched after all. . . .

The recognition that what we put out into the world matters, that our energy has influence and holds possibility, means that blessing your children—and all the kids at school—when you drop them off has consequences. Sending love to the postal worker or the grocery clerk has consequences. Intending to have a great day with your colleagues at work has consequences. Each of these simple, personal actions holds the promise of making the world a better place by focusing our energy in the right direction.

"There are so many opportunities to flood your mind with good thoughts throughout the day," Louise says. "And it can be so simple. As you go about your day, smile and say things to yourself like:

I love my life.

I love this day.

Life loves me.

I love it when the sun shines.

It is wonderful to feel the love in my heart.

Everything I do brings me joy.

"These thoughts will create a whole new experience for you."

Louise and I decide to brainstorm other ways to fill the day with good thoughts. Here are some of the ideas we come up with:

In the kitchen:

Louise tells me, "I always thank my stove for working well when I cook." So when *you* are in the kitchen, get in the habit of thanking your appliances. Thank your dishwasher, the blender, your teapot, the refrigerator, and so on, and use these affirmations while there:

Hello, kitchen, you are my nourishment center. I appreciate you!

You and all your appliances help me so much in easily preparing delicious, nutritious meals.

There is such an abundance of good, healthy food in my fridge.

I can easily make a delicious, nutritious meal.

You help me be cheerful.

I love you.

During meals:

Since we all have to eat, you can associate positive affirmations with every meal:

I am so grateful to have this wonderful food.

I bless this meal/food with love.

I love selecting foods that are nutritious and delicious.

The whole family is enjoying this meal.

Mealtime is laughter time. Laughter is good for the digestion.

Planning healthy meals is a joy.

My body loves the way I choose the perfect foods for every meal.

I am so fortunate that I can select healthy foods for my family.

We are all now nourished in preparation for the day before us.

In this house, all our meals are harmonious.

We gather together with great joy and love.

Mealtimes are happy times.

The kids love to try new foods.

My body heals and strengthens with every bite I take.

While doing laundry:

Choose three or four of your favorite affirmations from this book, tape them to the washer and dryer, and repeat them to yourself while doing the laundry.

Throughout the day:

Take 30 seconds to relax your shoulders and close your eyes. Inhale deeply through your nose as you count to four. Hold your breath for two counts, and then exhale slowly through your mouth for four counts. End by opening your eyes and sending a loving thought to someone.

In addition, get in the habit of asking yourself two questions throughout the day: *How can I make myself happy in this moment?* and *What thoughts bring me joy?*

When on the computer:

Turn the passwords on your computer into positive affirmations. I tell Louise about a friend who started doing this after going through a tough divorce. He realized that many of his passwords were associated with his ex, so he changed them to empowering messages. Just imagine how good you'd feel if you logged in with something like "ilovelife" as your password.

"You can also use affirmations to learn something new or to work on a particular area of your life," Louise adds. "Years ago I remember putting up signs with affirmations like: *I prosper wherever I turn,* and *My income is constantly increasing.* I'm very visual, and it was good to see them every day. After a while they became true."

So we want to squeeze in affirmations anywhere we can?

"There's always time for an affirmation," she agrees with a wink. "I even have an affirmation opposite my toilet that reads: *I bless and prosper everyone in my world, and everyone in my world blesses and prospers me.* I've had it there for a long time."

Louise and I enjoy a leisurely dinner, and when we finish, we walk home and decide to retire early.

I wake up feeling rested, and head out to the kitchen to make myself a cup of tea while reciting a few affirmations quietly to myself. I sit on a sofa in the living room, waiting for the sun to rise behind a mountain range I see in the distance. I note how comfortable it is here.

A little later, Louise comes downstairs with one of the books she keeps by her bed—Alan Cohen's *A Deep Breath of Life*. She hands it to me and says, "This is the book I mentioned the last time we talked. Have a look." As I'm about to turn to the first page, she instructs, "Open to a random page and see what the book has to say to you." Then she leaves.

I close my eyes, take a deep breath, and open to a page in the middle of the book. I feel an immediate chill as I read the title of the daily passage: "A Place for God." The entry is about establishing an altar in your home—a place where the presence of God can be remembered and honored. I'm struck by a moment of synchronicity. For the last month I'd been talking to my husband about taking over a small room in our home to create an altar—something I'd really missed since moving from our previous place where we had one. I see this passage in Alan's book as a clear sign that I need to make it a priority.

I join Louise at the island in her kitchen and comment on the number of sitting areas around her apartment. "It's important to pay attention to how we set up our home or work environment—where we spend most of our time," she explains. "I love different places to sit, and I love different views. I have a chaise lounge in my bedroom for reading, and a window seat for thinking. I make sure I have spaces in the garden, the kitchen, the living room, and my bedroom. I even make sure I have a comfortable place to sit when working with my assistant, Shelley, in her office."

It's clear that Louise sets things up in her life with intention *and* attention to detail. For years I learned to tolerate my environment either because I felt I couldn't afford to change it, or because I was so exhausted and overwhelmed that I didn't have the energy. Early in my training as a coach, my first mentor emphasized the importance of living and working in an environment that fueled me. That's when I started to take the idea seriously. I eliminated clutter, kept my home and office clean and organized, and got rid of anything I didn't love or need.

Yet seeing Louise's attention to detail—making sure every view is pleasant whether from her desk or her kitchen table, for instance—brings this idea to another level. Sometimes all it takes is a small change to send a big message to yourself that says, "I love you, and I care about what you need."

Louise gives me a tour of the upstairs of her home where the offices are located. When we step into hers, I see affirmations strategically placed around her desk and find what appears to be a makeup mirror attached to an accordion lamp by her computer. "Is this where you put your makeup on?" I ask.

Louise turns around and looks a bit surprised. "Now why would I put makeup on at my desk? That's for mirror work. I have them throughout the house so I can give myself positive messages during the day."

There's rarely a moment of prolonged embarrassment in Louise's company. Her loving, nonjudgmental way makes it impossible to feel foolish for too long. So, feeling just a little silly, I ask her to tell me more about how she uses her mirrors.

"Doing mirror work is very, very important," she replies. "It only takes a second to say 'Hi, kid,' or 'Looking good,' or 'Isn't this fun!' It's *so* important to give yourself little messages throughout the day. The more we use mirrors for complimenting ourselves, approving of ourselves, or supporting ourselves during difficult times, the more we develop a deeper and more enjoyable relationship with ourselves. The mirror needs to become a companion, a friend instead of an enemy."

I remember the days when the idea of becoming your own best friend sounded like a silly motivational slogan, but now I know it's crucial that we do so. Most of us are so hard on ourselves. As I look back on my own life, I can see that for years I made the mistake of believing that I could actually motivate myself to make positive changes by beating myself up—the old "kick in the ass" mentality. Now I see this for what it really is—a way of reinforcing limiting beliefs that keep us frightened and stuck.

As I've incorporated mirror work into my life, I've learned a valuable lesson in what it means to stand up for myself in any situation. Over the last few years, the habit of looking into a mirror and talking to myself in a kind, loving, and supportive way has made a huge impact on my relationship with myself. I've come to know—*really know*—that I have a trusted friend in me, and that I will stand by me regardless of what I do, mistakes and all. This practice has given me the freedom to step outside my comfort zone and expand my life in new and exciting ways.

"When something good happens in your life, you want to go to the mirror and say, 'Thank you, thank you. That's terrific! Thank you for doing this,'" Louise continues. "Or if something awful happens to you, you want to go to the mirror and say, 'It's okay, I love you. This thing will pass, but I love you and that's forever.' We need to support ourselves with our words instead of tearing ourselves down. We tear ourselves down far too much—that's the voice of someone else we heard when we were children."

Ah yes, the voice of the "internalized parent"—the guardians or authority figures from our past who projected their own fear or self-hatred onto us. Many of us grew up hearing about what we didn't do right, for example, or we've been taught to protect ourselves by minimizing our talents and gifts to avoid being told, "You're getting a big head." The practice of promoting growth with constant criticism is universal, and we end up taking these harsh voices in and making them our own. Our parents did the same thing, by the way. The critical voices are generational, and the truth is that by listening to and obeying them, we stop ourselves from expressing our full potential.

"This is why you need to be your own best cheerleader," Louise says. "You can't expect other people to do it. If you're a cheerleader for yourself, it's easier to try new things."

After our mirror lesson, Louise leads me back downstairs, where we continue our discussion about how to get ahold of the day. I grab my recorder and laptop and place them on the island in the kitchen where I can watch Louise as she makes breakfast. I want to talk about bringing awareness and good intentions to work. After all, most of us spend so much of our lives there. And it's where we're provided with plenty of opportunities to confront negative thinking and to practice good-feeling thoughts and actions. It turns out that Louise has a lot to say about the topic.

"Years ago I wrote a piece about blessing our work, and in it I shared some of the positive things people could do to feel better about their jobs," she tells me.

"Over the years I've seen plenty of people improve the quality of their workday regardless of whether they felt stuck, bored, frustrated, or unappreciated.

"The most powerful tool that I can share with you to transform any situation is the power of blessing with love," she emphasizes. "No matter where you work or how you feel about the place, bless it with love. I mean this literally. Don't just think positive thoughts in a vague way. Instead, say, 'I bless this job with love.' Find a place where you can say this out loud—there is so much power in giving voice to love. And don't stop there. Bless everything in your workplace with love: the equipment, the furniture, the machines, the products, the customers, the people you work with and for, and anything else associated with your job. It works wonders."

I take a moment to consider what I'd bless in my own office, the little things that serve me every day—my favorite desk, my computer, the windows that make a beautiful frame for an equally beautiful view, or the pens I write with all day long. Then I think about the bigger, more important things: my assistants, Chris and Nicole, such kind and loving women; my dear bookkeeper, Robin, who handles every detail with grace and ease; and my webmaster, Terry, who really is masterful at what she does. I feel fortunate to work in collaboration with individuals I respect and admire because I know from experience that workplace relationships can be quite challenging. Over the years, I've received thousands of requests for help in dealing with disgruntled co-workers, employees, or employers—so I ask Louise to share her thoughts about these relationships.

"If you have a difficult time with someone at work, you can use your mind to change the situation," she responds. "Affirmations work very well for this. Try: *I have a wonderful relationship with everyone at work, including* ___________. Every time that person comes into your mind, repeat the affirmation. On your way to work, affirm things like: *I am surrounded by wonderful co-workers, All my co-workers are just a delight to be with,* or *We have so much fun together.* Regardless of what's going on, that's what you keep saying. And when you find yourself saying anything else, just stop yourself and say: 'No, no, no, I have a wonderful relationship with all of my co-workers.' Whenever they come up in your mind, especially the ones you have trouble with, focus on what's right with them instead of what's wrong. You will be amazed by how the relationship improves. I've seen things you can't even imagine happen. Just speak the words, and let the Universe sort out the details."

I ask Louise if she can think of a story from her own life that would demonstrate this kind of miracle, with respect to good relationships with co-workers. She has a great one at the ready.

"I remember having a client named George years ago, who had a new job coming up—he was a pianist in a nightclub. During our first meeting he said, 'I'm excited about my new job, but the only problem is that the boss has a horrible reputation with employees. Everybody's afraid of him. They hide from him, and people even tell me they hate him. I wonder what I'm going to do.'

"So I told him, 'Okay, first of all, as you're going toward the building, bless it with love. If there are elevators or doors, bless them with love. If you have a dressing room, bless it with love. Bless the whole place with love, including every employee in it, and affirm that you have an absolutely wonderful relationship with your boss. Keep affirming: *I have a wonderful relationship with my boss.* And whenever you leave the building, continue to bless it with love.'

"Within six weeks he came to me and said, 'Everyone is amazed. The boss really likes me. He's always coming up and saying, "Hi, George, how're you doing? You're doing a great job." And he's even slipped me $20 bills now and then [which was a lot of money at that time]. All the other employees are shocked. They keep asking: "What in the hell are you doing?"'

"You see, it worked for George. The boss was mean to everyone else and yet great to him."

As I listen to Louise tell the story, I realize that this is a good example of how easy it is to get co-opted into the history of others. Like George, so many of us walk into something new—a job, a neighborhood, a volunteer group, or a class—and buy into the stories of the people we join rather than program the types of experiences we'd most like to have.

As Louise explains, "Sometimes we take our history with us. If you hate the job you have now, for example, there is a danger that you will take that hatred with you when you move to a new one. However good the new job is, you will soon find yourself hating it, too. Whatever feelings or thoughts you have within you now will be carried to the new place. *If you live within a world of discontentment, you will find it wherever you go. Only by changing your consciousness will you start to see positive results in your life.*

"If you absolutely hate your current job, try this affirmation: *I always love where I work. I have the best jobs. I am always appreciated.* If you do so, then when a new one comes along, it will be good and you will be able to really enjoy it. By continually affirming this, you'll be creating a new personal law for yourself, and the Universe will respond in kind. Like attracts like, and Life will always look for ways to bring good to you if you allow it.

"If you'd like to get a new job, then in addition to blessing your current one, try this affirmation: *I release this job to the next person, who will be so glad to be here.* That particular job was ideal for you at the time you got it. Now your sense of self-worth has grown, and you're ready to move on to better things. Your affirmations are:

I accept a job that uses all my creative talents and abilities.

This job is deeply fulfilling, and it is a joy for me to go to work each day.

I work for people who appreciate me.

The building where I work is light, bright, and airy; and filled with a feeling of enthusiasm.

My new job is in the perfect location and I earn good money, for which I am deeply grateful."

So we're placing ourselves in good situations by first placing ourselves in good situations in our minds?

"Yes, you want to be the person who does the positive affirmations and hears about friends who have problems, rather than the friend who *has* the problems. You're placing yourself in life experiences with every thought you think—and once you realize that, you can do so much more with your life."

We decide to take a break at this point, since we need to get ready for the day. We're going to the Hay House corporate office in Carlsbad, just north of San Diego, for a lunch meeting and to visit with employees.

Louise and I walk down to the garage, toward her car. When I get into the passenger side, I grin as I read an affirmation stuck on the console: *Smile with your liver.* For a moment I imagine a giant yellow smiley face plastered across my liver, keeping it happy and healthy.

On our drive to Hay House, I flip the conversation from being an employee to being an employer. I wonder about ways to positively impact the workplace when you're the one running the show.

"If you're an employer, it's so important to thank your employees," she tells me. "People love receiving small notes from time to time, or a hug, or some acknowledgment of a job well done. It makes everyone feel good."

So the old idea of "ruling with an iron fist" doesn't work? I ask in mock seriousness.

"*Never!* I don't understand bosses who think that if they yell at their employees, they'll do better work. They won't, because they're now frightened or resentful, and you cannot do good work when you feel like that.

If you're a boss, you need to be aware of what you're doing to your employees. 'Well, I'll make them work harder!' That doesn't make people work harder, it makes them work frightened."

It's obvious to me that Louise cares deeply about the people who work for her company. When we get to the office, one of the first things she has planned to do is to participate in a thank-you video for an employee who's leaving Hay House after many years of service. I ask her what she's going to say.

"I intend to say, 'We love you. We want you to go off and have a fabulous life. Thank you for being here. You were really helpful. Go forth and have new adventures like you've never had before,'" she replies. "I say this a lot when writing notes: *May your life continue to grow and expand.*"

Who wouldn't be energized or feel cared for and confident with these kinds of messages from an employer? Who wouldn't want to work hard and contribute to the success of the company? Ongoing positive feedback is a rarity in the workplace. So many of us never received positive endorsements when growing up, so it doesn't even occur to us to give them to others now as adults.

My first life coach was a stickler for acknowledging clients. He had me put several 3" × 5" index cards around my office with the words *Endorse! Endorse! Endorse!* on each one. He wanted me to have a constant reminder to be a strong champion for my clients' strengths and success. Clearly, it's a skill that needs to be developed and practiced—especially by employers. They have so much to gain from these types of daily habits.

Back at Hay House, Louise shows me around, and I enjoy seeing the faces of the men and women I work with, most of whom I'd only known by phone or e-mail up to this point. There are so many good people at this company who care about the products they put out into the world—books, events, online programs, movies, and other tools that have such a life-changing, positive impact on their customers.

Throughout the afternoon, as Louise and I go in and out of meetings and conversations, she maintains a positive, upbeat attitude. I can't get over the amount of energy she has at 84 years old!

At the end of our day, I stop in to say good-bye to my production team at Hay House Radio. Their offices are located near the reception area of the building, and I keep an eye out for Louise, who will meet me at the front door.

While standing just inside the studio, I see her come around the corner, deep in conversation with an employee—a young man who looks to be in his early 30s. As they finish up, I watch as she hugs him and says,

"I love you." I shake my head and marvel, *What boss does that in corporate America?*

When the workday is done, coming home has its own set of thought patterns. So, on the drive back to Louise's place, she completes our daily plan. "Once again, we need to ask ourselves, how do I feel when I get home? How do I feel when I see my partner, my children, or my roommate?

"I remember, long ago, spending time with a friend who used to greet her husband with the latest disaster, and as I watched her, I thought, *Why do you do that?* When I was married, I always made sure that when my husband walked in the door, I greeted him with a hug and a kiss and a welcoming attitude. Instead, my friend gave her husband bad news—the toilet won't work or the kids have been crazy. Now, that news could have waited 80 seconds and been delivered after 'Hi, honey, I love you. How was your day?'"

Just as when we leave the house at the beginning of the day, we want to bring our awareness to the thoughts we think when we get home. Take a second to ask yourself: *How do I feel when I pull into my driveway? How do I feel when I walk up to the door? What's the first thing I say to others or myself when I walk inside?*

Of course, Louise has some affirmations for approaching the door:

Good evening, house, I am back home.

I am so glad to be here. I love you.

Let us have a great evening together.

I am looking forward to seeing my family.

We have a lovely time together tonight.

The kids whiz through their homework in no time.

Dinner seems to make itself.

"Do you look forward to your evening at home?" Louise continues. "If so, why? If not, why not? What are you thinking about when you're making dinner or getting takeout? Is dinner a joyful event, or is it something that frustrates you or makes you feel irritable? Do you grab the worst possible—fast or processed—food, or food that nourishes you? How do you talk to yourself when you're cleaning up? Do you look forward to going to bed?"

I smile when I hear her last question. I always look forward to going to bed. When my workday is done, I straighten up my desk, make plans for the next morning, and shut the door. Having a clear end to the workday is important.

When it's time to go to sleep, I think of the bedroom as my sanctuary—a place of rejuvenation and healing. Whenever anyone asks me for my secret to success, a good night's sleep is always near the top of the list. I thrive on it, at least eight hours a night, and I've made a point to really honor what my body needs to get good rest.

I use a few simple guidelines to get the sleep I need:

- Go to bed at the same time (a reasonable hour) every night.
- Keep TV out of the bedroom.
- Make sure the room is dark and a bit cool.
- Don't have any food or caffeine at least three or four hours before I sleep.
- Use soft, comfortable sheets.
- Slip into a bed warmed by a heating pad (then the pad is shut off and unplugged).
- Read a good book to get sleepy.

I admit to Louise that while I normally keep all electronics out of the bedroom, every now and then I'll get pulled in to a news story and end up reading about it on my phone while in bed. She has an immediate reaction: "No, no, no! Seeing the news just before you go to sleep takes all that negativity into your dream world. I am so against people watching or reading the news in bed!"

But I prefer to get my news online from places where I can monitor what I'll see, I tell her. I am very sensitive and don't like violent news or stories that leave me feeling helpless or unsettled.

"I don't care what the news is," Louise cuts in. "You need to be mindful of what you're putting into your consciousness before you go to sleep. I feel strongly about this."

Once again I'm reminded that good self-care begins with caring for our thoughts. It's so easy to ignore or minimize even the occasional habits that may be putting our emotional or mental health at risk. Listening to Louise's passionate take on being exposed to the news before bed convinces me to stop reading it right then and there. Instead, I'll stick to placing my attention on a good book from now on.

"I love reading stories that touch my heart, human-interest stories or something inspirational," she says. "Reading takes precedence over anything else. I don't watch much TV anyway. To me, television is newfangled —it's not what I was raised with.

"Often I listen to meditation CDs before going to bed and may even fall asleep to them on a low volume. I usually do a blessing—a thank-you for the day and for what I've accomplished. Then I greet my bed and get ready to go to sleep. Sometimes I revisit the day in my mind, but not always. The day is done."

In preparation for the close of the day and to finish the topic of living more consciously throughout the day, I ask Louise if she performs any type of ritual before drifting off to sleep.

"I take a few deep breaths as I close my eyes. Then, on the in-breath, I say, 'Life,' and on the out-breath, 'loves me.' I repeat it several times as I drift off to sleep: *'Life loves me, Life loves me, Life loves me.'"*

A great ending indeed . . .

CHAPTER FIVE

Don't Break a Habit —Dissolve It!

We're lost.

My husband, Michael, and I are on our way to the Wizarding World of Harry Potter in Orlando, Florida, with our good friend Ileen. I'm speaking at a conference in the area over the weekend, which will allow me the chance to meet with Louise. And the three of us have decided to sneak off and spend the day entertaining our inner kids before the conference begins.

The drive has taken much longer than we anticipated, and we're almost out of gas—literally and emotionally. We got a late start after waiting for the rental-car paperwork to be finalized, and there are now only a few short hours left before the park closes. When Michael, Ileen, and I finally arrive, we drive through the gated entrance and attempt to follow the directions to the parking lot. The signs are confusing, and my husband and I briefly argue about which way to go.

I point in one direction, hoping that I'm right, and no sooner does he make the turn than it becomes obvious I'm not. So, with eyes ever mindful of the empty fuel tank, we're led back onto the highway, heading away from the park without a turnaround (or gas station) in sight. At this point, Michael and I are pretty pissed at each other, but we're too polite to say anything in the company of our friend.

The tension of unspoken anger hangs like a heavy drape between us as my ego firmly grabs hold of the situation. *I know I pointed in the right direction, but the signs were confusing. If Michael had paid attention, we wouldn't be in this mess. He always waits for me to make decisions. Why didn't he just make the choice himself?* On and on my mind goes, mentally chewing the situation to pieces. I'm convinced that I'm right. Meanwhile, I know Michael well enough to realize that he's busy kicking himself for not trusting his gut and taking the turn he knew he should have taken. Ileen, smart gal that she is, is stone silent in the backseat, patiently waiting for us to unravel this mess.

As I sit there fuming, I think of Louise and the conversations we've had about choosing good thoughts. For a fraction of a second, a door cracks open in my mind and I see a glimmer of light. I consider a different approach. Rather than redecorate hell by arguing about who did what (a practice pointed out to Michael and me by a helpful therapist long ago), I take a chance. I reach over, place my hand on Michael's, and mentally send him love. I don't say a word. And he doesn't move his hand.

I look straight ahead at the road and visualize love flowing from a Divine Source down through my body, out of my hand to his, and then into his heart. I keep this practice going for several minutes, when I feel Michael's energy soften. As I continue to send him love, I notice something interesting. I feel love, too. Instead of fuming about the wrong turn, I'm suddenly more concerned about my husband. My heart softens as I imagine how he must be beating himself up. Why would I want to heap more pain on top of that?

As I send love to Michael, I can feel his defenses relax . . . and before I know it, we come upon a gas station and a turnaround. Thirty minutes later we're laughing and joking as we enter the park, ready to meet Muggles, magicians, and—who knows?—maybe even Harry Potter himself.

When I next meet up with Louise, I share my Harry Potter story. I tell her I'm still surprised by how something so simple could have such a profound effect on our day. So many times, in the middle of some silly argument (and some not so silly), I'd entertain the thought of dropping my defenses and listening with love, but it felt so counterintuitive—like giving in. After all, my ego is masterful at rationalizing a position. Why admit defeat when I've done nothing wrong? Isn't sending love just ignoring the problem? And how are we going to challenge each other to grow if we're not willing to take a stand for what we know to be true?

"The ego has one agenda," Louise tells me now. "It wants to be right, and it has a habit of trying to justify its position. It searches for an angle where the other person is clearly wrong. It's a simple idea to think that focusing on a positive outcome or putting love into the situation could work, but it does. In your case, instead of affirming the problem by continuing to complain or argue, you just smiled inwardly, sent your husband love, and discovered that it works!"

While I was aware of the resistance I had to surrendering my ego, I had to admit that Louise was right. It *did* work.

"Too often we feel like we need to grind everything we can out of a problem," she continues. "We want to find the solution, *now!* I don't like dealing with problems that way anymore. The more you can turn away from a problem, the quicker the solution comes. That's why I love the affirmation *All is well. Everything is working out for my highest good. Out of this situation only good will come. I am safe.* It lifts you totally up and out of the problem into an area where there are solutions. In this place, you're not telling Life how to create the solution—you're just affirming that it's working for everybody.

"Your situation with Michael while driving in the car is a wonderful example because you did so little. You could have argued with him for the rest of the day and you would have both been miserable."

That's for sure. And the truth is that we actually invite positive changes into our relationships when we're soft and open enough to listen. In fact, later that evening, when Michael and I returned to the hotel after visiting the park, we were able to talk about the situation calmly and constructively. Over the years, we've both learned that when there is defensiveness, there is no communication. Nada. No way. Not a chance. We've also learned that it's important to let something go once we've worked through it in a loving way. Bringing it up again or complaining about it after the fact is an invitation for trouble.

"When a problem has been solved, we need to remember that it's gone," Louise instructs. "It has passed. *We don't want to dip into the past to be miserable in the present moment.* And we don't want to become complainers. People who complain a lot are a pain in the ass for everyone around them. Not only that, but they are doing great damage to their own world. Before we verbalize a complaint, we tend to go over it in our mind—several times, dozens of times, several dozen times, dozens and dozens of times. Depending on what our habit is."

At this point I cringe inside as I think about the amount of energy I've expended over the years complaining about everything from how busy I am to what Michael does or doesn't do. Before understanding the power of my own thoughts, I had allowed this "inner complainer," a chronically irritated gal, to have free rein over my mind and mouth. She constantly griped about the same things over and over again, as if whining about them would somehow make things better.

"Most people have created a habit of constantly complaining in their mind," Louise tells me. "Each time we do this, it is an affirmation, a very negative affirmation. The more we complain, the more we find to complain about. Life always gives us what we concentrate on. The more we concentrate on what is wrong in our life, the more wrongs we will find. The more wrongs we find, the more miserable we will become. It's an endless cycle. We become a constant victim of Life."

And that's when we feel like we're stuck in a rut, I add. Once again, that's when we need to get back in the driver's seat and take charge of our thinking.

"Yes. The only person who can stop this negative landslide is the person who is doing the complaining. But first they have to recognize *what* they're doing. Second, they have to recognize *when* they're doing it. It is only when we recognize that we're saying a negative affirmation that we can make the change. As people drop this self-damaging habit, they will watch themselves move from being victims to being conscious creators of their lives.

"Whether the habit we want to dissolve is complaining or something else, it is the same process. Notice I said *dissolve,* not *break*. When we break something, the pieces are still around. *When we dissolve something, the whole experience disappears.* I like to think it goes back to the nothingness from whence it came. Habits come from nowhere, and they can go back to nowhere. We all have habits. Some of them really support us, and some are letting us down. We want to select the ones that will contribute to creating love and joy; prosperity; good health; and a happy, peaceful mind."

So we need to remember who created the habits we live with now, and who's in charge of changing them.

"Yes. If there is anything negative in our lives, we want to find out how *we* are contributing to holding it in place. What are we doing to attract and maintain the negative conditions in our world? We are all powerful creators who create continuously. My experience has taught me that it is vital to a happy life that we become consciously aware of the negative chatter in our minds. What are we thinking? Why are we thinking this thought? What is this thought creating for us in our world?

"Once you notice this habit, the next step is to stop beating yourself up for thinking these thoughts. Instead, become delighted to notice what you're doing. You could tell yourself, *No wonder I'm having this negative reaction—it's because I'm thinking this negative thought. Now I want to become aware of every time I do it so I can dissolve the habit.* And the next time you catch yourself doing it, say, *Oh, caught myself again, that's great; it is part of the dissolving process. I'm getting there.* We want to rejoice when we're in the process of dissolving a negative habit. The idea is to stay in the present or look toward the future with a positive outlook as much as possible."

My driving debacle with Michael is an example of the kinds of everyday challenges we all face as we move through life. As we bring more intention to how we live our days, it's important to keep in mind that we will get thrown off track by old habits, beliefs, and circumstances, especially when we're under stress. Louise and I go on to discuss a few of the common habits that need to be dissolved—the kinds of obstacles that get people into trouble. The first one has to do with money.

Each week I host a live Internet radio show, *Coach on Call,* where I provide coaching for people all over the world. I frequently receive phone calls from those who believe that starting a business will bring them a quick financial fix, or that winning the lottery is what they need to finally feel secure and happy. They are mired in "magical thinking," believing in a future fantasy that ultimately keeps them stuck.

"So many people think that all they need to be happy and to fix all their problems is money," Louise says. "But we know that there are thousands of people who have a great deal of wealth and still have plenty of problems. Clearly money does not fix everything. We all want to be happy and to enjoy peace of mind, but happiness and well-being are an *inside* job. You can have both and still have very little money. It is all about the thoughts you choose to think. The rich or poor conditions you create inside of you.

"The amount of money we allow ourselves to have has everything to do with our belief system and what we learned about money as a child. Many women, for instance, find it difficult to earn more money than their fathers. The beliefs *I can't out-succeed my dad* or *Only men earn high salaries* hold them back, even though they may not be consciously aware of it. And, yes, there is also a belief that insists, *If I win the lottery, all my troubles will be over.* This is nonsense. In less than a year or two, almost everyone who wins the lottery is worse off than before they won it. That's because they did not have a change of consciousness to go with their new wealth. They may not have had the skills to manage their newfound wealth, but they also didn't believe that they were deserving of the money they'd won.

"The more we choose to believe in an abundant Universe, the more we find that our needs are met. The affirmation *Life loves me, and all my needs are met at all times,* will start us on the process."

I tell Louise that I remember struggling with my own financial fears in my early 30s. I was living alone, trying to grow my business as a professional speaker, and constantly worrying about paying the bills. I was so anxious most of the time that all I could do was focus on the problem: no money. Rather than assuage my fear with a fantasy of overnight success or a lottery windfall, I was convinced that if I just worried enough, my circumstances would somehow magically change.

"When we worry, we repeat our worries over and over again until we have thoroughly frightened ourselves," she replies. "Too many of us scare ourselves with our thoughts. But miracles occur when we repeat our positive affirmations as often as, or more often than, our worries. This is how our negative conditions begin to turn around, no matter what the problem."

I did my best during that time of my life to stay focused on positive affirmations, yet I found it difficult to sustain the practice while feeling so anxious. That's when I learned something important: affirmations *and* appropriate action are the keys to success. When I finally faced the fact that I needed to get a job, *and* I started looking for one, I was suddenly working *in cooperation* with Life. That's when circumstances began to change. I used the affirmation *The perfect job finds me* as a continual mantra, and started networking like crazy. By putting myself in a determined and focused state of mind, I discovered that Life brought me the resources, people, and opportunities I needed to turn my situation around.

"If we are willing to do the work of changing our consciousness by changing our thoughts *and* acting accordingly, then we are able to create a new life for ourselves that is far grander than anything the lottery could bring us," Louise says. "Then, as we reach new levels of success, we'll be able to sustain it because we've now had a change of consciousness and our belief systems have been updated. But remember, while everyone thinks being wealthy will make them happy, that's not where happiness comes from. If you can't love yourself, if you can't forgive, if you can't be grateful, money won't help. You'll just have more servants to yell at."

Louise and I talk about a few of the steps everyone can take to dissolve the habits related to poor financial health. First, focus on feeling deserving and worthy of abundance so you can invite *and* receive more prosperity into your life. You can use affirmations such as:

I gratefully accept all the good I have in my life now.

Life loves me and provides for me.

I trust Life to take care of me.

I am worthy of abundance.

Life always provides for my needs.

Abundance flows into my life in surprising ways every day.

My income is constantly increasing.

I prosper wherever I turn.

Choose one or two of these, and repeat them over and over throughout the day. Write them down several times in a journal or on a piece of paper, make them into signs and hang them around your home or office, and be sure to repeat them to yourself while looking into a mirror every chance you get.

Writing can be a wonderful way to access wisdom and insight. So take some time to explore the following question in a journal or notebook:

What one habit do I need to dissolve to create the financial life I want?

If you set aside some time to explore this question, you might discover that you're living in the future, more focused on the good things that *might* happen, rather than on the reality of what needs to get handled right now. Or you may need to step out of denial and stop pretending that you can continue to spend money when you're unable to take care of the expenses you already have.

Finally, identify the one step you most need to take to improve your financial health. Then focus on this one action—preferably the one you've been avoiding—and do something about it within the next 24 hours. You might need to pay your bills, file your taxes, or stop using your credit cards. Or you may need to look for any job that will bring money into your household as soon as possible so you can prepare yourself for more satisfying work later on. Remember, when you affirm your intentions *and* take action, you align yourself with Universal energy, inviting Life to rise up and meet you. (If you're not sure what step to take, ask a trusted friend or family member for advice—someone who knows you intimately and has your best interest at heart.)

Here's another common problem many of us need to work on: wishing and hoping that those around us will finally "get it" and change.

What do you do when someone keeps struggling yet won't do anything to change the situation? I was once leading a workshop, when I opened the floor for questions about where these women felt stuck in relation to their self-care. One woman in her mid-40s immediately grabbed the microphone and began to tell us about her drama-filled life. It seems that every time she turned around, another crisis materialized in her life. The latest had to do with work. She had been falsely accused of harassing a fellow employee and was now panicked about losing her job.

As she launched into the details of the situation, I was able to empathize with her plight—and I could tell that she had far more of her energy wrapped up in the problem than the solution. So I stopped her and suggested that she try something different. "Why not begin to turn things around by shifting your language?" I advised. "For example, you could start by affirming: *I enjoy a peaceful resolution to this problem. The uncomfortable situation at work is resolved quickly, and everyone feels content with the outcome.* Or try: *I release all drama from my life and now get energy from peace."*

"I can't possibly do that," she piped up with a pronounced edge of irritation in her voice. "My co-worker is an idiot, and she's not telling the truth."

For several minutes we did the ego dance, with me trying to find an opening in her frightened mind to allow her to approach the situation in a new way, and her struggling to convince me why it wouldn't work. I knew the drill. This woman was used to getting energy from drama, and in the past I would have spent far too much time trying to get her to change her mind. But because I recognized the dance, I knew I needed to allow her to continue to make herself right until she was ready to shift her perspective. I bowed out graciously and moved on to another question.

Louise explains, "That's what happens when people aren't ready to change. You can only make suggestions for how someone might support their own growth, but ultimately they need to be willing to do the work. We need to stop wanting people to do what they can't do, or be who they can't be. I've always said that I am not a salesperson. I'm not here to sell a way of life. I'm a teacher. If you want to come and learn from me, I'm happy to teach you—but I'm not going to force you to change your mind. That's your privilege. You have the freedom to believe anything you want to, and if you want to take a step in this direction and explore it, then fine, but if you don't, do your thing.

"We are all under the law of our own consciousness. Therefore, any problem is created at the level of consciousness of the person involved. *Your* consciousness can't change the situation; their consciousness needs to change. The woman at your workshop will continue to draw drama into her life until she recognizes that *she* is influencing these situations. It's not *them* out there—*we* are creating this in our world. It's her thoughts and beliefs that are contributing to the problem.

"It's such a shame because when people dismiss affirmations or decide that doing the kinds of things we're talking about are silly or unlikely to work, they just experience the same problems over and over again. Then they say that affirmations don't work. They *do* work. They just need to be used consistently."

Our thoughts directly influence our life experience. In this way, we're contributing to everything that occurs in our lives. If we find ourselves in the middle of trouble, we need to reach for new habits that use our thoughts and energy in a more productive way. Affirmations help point us in a new direction so we can focus on a better outcome.

"And the key is to catch ourselves as quickly as possible rather than get pulled into the drama of the moment," Louise remarks. "Remember, we need to stop and say, 'Oh, look at what *I'm* doing to myself. It's not about the other person. It's about me. What can I do, *right now,* to shift the energy?' While the other person may be doing something to us or to the situation, *we* control how we respond and react. We need to always keep in mind that the goal in life is to feel good, as much as we can."

When dealing with this woman at the workshop, I was ultimately able to let her go on her way. But, I ask Louise, what if someone is intimately involved with another person who's not ready to change? They might be dealing with an aging parent who is always negative, for example, or a spouse who isn't on the same path of self-discovery. How would they make peace with that situation?

"Many years ago, when I worked with people who had AIDS, I found that so many of them had been abandoned by their parents. Totally abandoned. From the moment a parent found out that their child was a homosexual, they were banished from the family. A lot of it had to do with what the neighbors would think.

"When this happened, I would tell the men I worked with to use a version of an affirmation I mentioned earlier: *I have a wonderful, harmonious relationship with everyone in my family, especially my mother* (this was usually the person they struggled with the most).

"I suggested that they repeat this affirmation several times throughout the day. Every time the person came into their minds, they needed to keep repeating the affirmation. Now, in the face of being abandoned by their family, this certainly wasn't what anyone expected to be asked to do. But invariably, between three to six months after using this affirmation continually, a mother would agree to come to a meeting with her son."

No kidding? I ask, both surprised and moved.

"Yes." Louise stops for a moment to revisit this memory, and I watch as tears well up in her eyes. "And when she did show up, we would give her a standing ovation. It meant a lot to us. It was so healing. Dads were a little harder to get in, but Mom would be there, and she'd find that these 'homosexuals' would give her so much love.

"So you could say that it's crazy to think an affirmation could do something in such a difficult situation. What could it possibly do? How could it influence someone else's behavior? I don't know. It went out into the ethers, and instead of the person having terrible thoughts about their family, they started to create space where there could be a harmonious relationship. I don't know how this stuff works. That's the mystery of Life."

I suggest that affirming a harmonious relationship with others can be applied in a variety of ways, and Louise agrees. "Whether you train yourself to keep affirming that you have a harmonious relationship with your boss, your neighbor, a co-worker, or an estranged family member, it's got to play out," she says. *"Bypass the issue and talk about what you want, as though it is so.*

"No more focusing on *My mother was mean to me.* You don't want to get into that, because that's what you are then giving power to. You want to stay focused on the goal instead. And we're not even saying that she has to behave in a certain way. We're saying that *you* get along wonderfully with everyone in your family —including your mother—and then you let Life figure out how to put that together. You need to keep affirming this every time you think of the person or the problem. The more difficult the relationship, the more you need to repeat the affirmation."

When these types of things happen—when we struggle with a difficult family member, or feel blindsided by unexpected news like the diagnosis of an illness or the loss of a job—what's the fastest way to get back on track?

"First of all, you're allowed to have your initial reaction. You need to allow yourself to feel whatever you feel. When I talk about using affirmations, I'm not suggesting that you use them to avoid feeling your feelings."

This is such an important point, I note. Too often I see people attempting to use affirmations as a way of glossing over or avoiding the truth, as if they're trying to override their emotions with their head. But whenever anyone uses their head as a ruler over their heart, they put themselves at a disadvantage. Feelings actually provide valuable information.

If you're feeling overwhelmed by your job, it certainly would be helpful to affirm: *I feel peaceful and calm at work*. But it may also be an indication that you need to stop taking on extra projects as well. Or if you're feeling lonely in your marriage, you can hold the thought of a harmonious relationship, but you might also need to sit down with your spouse and talk about what's going on. When paid attention to, feelings let you know what is or isn't working in your life. Then they can point you in the direction of change. *Ultimately, it's the alignment of head and heart that creates the alchemy that gives your affirmations power.*

"Once you know what's going on and you've given yourself the chance to feel, you need to figure out how to get yourself out of the uncomfortable mental space as soon as possible," Louise says. "This is the time to remember that the quality of *this moment* is the most important point of creation. Right now. Every thought you think and every choice you make in this moment is setting your future in motion. So you want to put yourself in the right place. We need to truly understand the importance of that."

So rather than be pessimistic, we need to become hopeful as soon as possible?

"No. The way I see it, hope is another obstacle. Saying, 'I hope,' really means 'I don't believe.' It's like putting your desire in some far-distant future and believing that perhaps one day it *might* happen. That is not a positive affirmation. You need to create a positive, present-focused affirmation. And then you need to let go."

Let go?

"You let go. You stop hanging on. Don't suffer. When there's nothing more you can do about a situation, just let it go because you're only holding on to the past and to memories that are taking up too much room in your mind. So I would say, yes, definitely, choose affirmations and do them nonstop—try to find one or two that really comfort you and keep doing them and doing them. And if you can do mirror work, it helps a lot because you can really connect with yourself in that way. Look into a mirror whenever you can, and say to yourself, 'We are getting through this. I love you, and I'm here for you."

Just then I glance at the clock and realize that I need to leave for a meeting. Breaking the spell of the moment, I stand up and suggest that we meet later in the day, after Louise's book signing—a two-hour period where hundreds of fans from around the world will line up for photos and autographs.

As I put my notes into my bag, I turn to Louise with one last question: What about the things we can't control, the little negative events that push our buttons and keep us preoccupied throughout the day? You know, a mean-spirited e-mail or a comment from a jealous co-worker—how do you handle those types of interruptions?

"That's easy," she replies with a sly smile. *"I'm no longer curious about things that will upset me."*

Louise stares at me for several moments, her gaze locking in the message. I break eye contact, glance down at my phone, and tap the STOP button on the recorder. Imagine not getting pulled into the drama of someone else's agenda.

Now that's a habit worth dissolving.

CHAPTER SIX

The Beauty of Wisdom

It's a warm November day in Tampa, and Louise has just delivered the welcome address to more than 3,000 attendees of Hay House's "I Can Do It" conference. Standing at the side of the room, I watch as the sold-out crowd erupts in affectionate applause when she announces that she's in her ninth decade, and it's the best one of her life so far. It's such an inspiring moment.

On the way to our hotel, I study Louise as she walks purposefully toward the front door. A unique blend of funky and elegant, she's dressed in a flowery crinkled shirt draped over tight-fitting leggings. She radiates the energy of youth and the beauty of aged wisdom.

We arrive at the hotel and head up to Louise's room. She immediately opens the balcony doors, and I feel a comfortable breeze graze my skin while I scope out a place to sit. I flop down, cross-legged, on a wing-back chair near a stunning arrangement of flowers—lilies, tulips, sunflowers, and raspberry-colored roses—resting on the center of a coffee table in the middle of the room. "The flowers are a gift from someone who needed my help last week," she tells me. "They make me so happy."

She makes her way to the kitchenette and proceeds to make us each a cup of tea. While she removes the tea bags from their wrapping, she shares her excitement at having found a new black velvet cover for her iPad—the latest technology tool she's been enjoying with gusto. I realize that even at age 84, Louise is the eternal student. I so admire her curiosity and hunger for learning.

I set my tools around me and wonder what she knows at 84 about feeling comfortable in her skin that I could learn at 51. I ask her how she looks and feels so good at her age—what's her secret?

"Well, to me it comes down to loving yourself, loving your body, and making peace with the aging process," she replies. "You can't do anything well or for the long term without loving yourself first. When you love yourself, you care about your body, and you care about what you put into it. You also care about the thoughts you choose to think."

So if we're diligent about practicing what we've already talked about in this book, we'll have a much easier time as we age?

"Yes. Life has gotten much easier for me because I've learned how to plan my experiences. My positive affirmations go before me, smoothing the way. I make a point to anticipate what I would like to experience in the future. For instance, today I needed to do three errands, so I affirmed: *This is a glorious day, and every experience is a joyous adventure.*

"As I entered each of the three different stores, I found lovely salespeople who made friendly conversation with me. One clerk and I even laughed and laughed over something silly. Each of these experiences was a small yet joyous adventure. Part of the wisdom of aging is to find joy in even the simplest situations. When we live our lives to the fullest, we're going to make the little things in life wonderful and good and important."

I note that as we get older and lose friends or family members, it seems that we value our connection to others more, even the kind of connection Louise is talking about in these everyday situations.

"We could, or it could make us bitter. We can choose to be bitter about losing loved ones, or we can choose to reach out to new people and fill the emptiness."

The more I get to know Louise, the more I appreciate, on a deep level, the value of putting good thought habits in place early in life. When she talks about her approach to living, it's clear that she's invested a lot of time and energy in managing her mind. As a result, this investment has given her a far more positive view of aging. Her vigilance about living with purpose and intention keeps paying great dividends year after year. As I witness her response to life, I keep being reminded to deepen this habit myself.

"Don't get me wrong," Louise admits. "I've faced the same challenges most people do as they age—wrinkles, weight gain, stiffness, and noticing that young men no longer look longingly at me. But there's no use making myself miserable about things I cannot change. We're all going to age. I've just made a decision to take care of myself and love myself no matter what.

"I eat well. I consume foods that are very good for my body, foods that support me. I eat very little that drains my body or that doesn't support me. I also do things like acupuncture and craniosacral sessions once a month as a general tune-up. And I do my best to choose thoughts that make me feel good as much as possible. This is the big lesson that I'll keep repeating: *Our thinking either makes us feel good or it makes us feel bad.* It's not the events nearly as much as it's the thoughts."

So it's not the wrinkle, it's the thoughts you have about the wrinkle?

"Absolutely. The wrinkle is just there. And it's there for everybody. You haven't been singled out to be the one person who has that wrinkle. It's foolish to make yourself unhappy about something like that. We want to enjoy every phase of life as much as possible."

Speaking of wrinkles, I mention, let's talk about the body. You said that the secret to your success at 84 has to do with loving yourself and your body, but what if you're a woman who's 50 pounds overweight and hates what she sees in the mirror? How do you look at yourself and say "I love you" when you don't like what you see?

"Well, that's the point of what we're doing," Louise replies. "As I said before, I no longer believe in working on a single issue. In the early days, I worked with individual problems like weight loss. Then one day I discovered that if I could get clients to love themselves, we didn't have to work on problems anymore. Self-love was the core issue for everybody and everything. And that's a difficult realization for a lot of people to accept or acknowledge—that it could be that simple.

"This woman you're talking about might think her issue is weight, but it isn't her issue at all; it's self-hatred. If we can get to the bottom of that or get her to start consistently practicing affirmations that will support her in building a good relationship with her body, it will begin the process of self-love."

After pausing for a moment, she goes on. "It's true that sometimes you need to adjust your diet in order to stick with this new practice. By now, most of us know that sugar is addictive and just isn't good for the body. Wheat and dairy products cause problems for many people, too. We need to eat foods that nourish and fuel our body *and* our mind. While it's wonderful to say the right affirmations, if you're loading yourself up on caffeine, sugar, junk food, and the like, you're going to have a hard time focusing your mind on anything at all, let alone positive affirmations. And if you've grown up on junk food, then you might need some guidance on what it means to eat a healthy diet. I didn't know anything about good nutrition until my cancer diagnosis invited me to find out what my body needed. Even now I still keep up with the latest info when it comes to health and healing."

I can certainly appreciate the importance of taking good care of the body as we age. Like so many of us, I've read my share of books, websites, and studies trying to learn as much as I can about diet, exercise, or supplements. There is a maze of information out there, and it's easy to get confused. Our society spends billions of dollars on anti-aging books and products, health-club memberships, and diet programs, searching for the right formula for creating optimal health . . . yet obesity rates continue to climb, and our overall health continues to decline.

In the last several months, I'd been focusing on exactly what Louise is talking about: loving myself and my body *first,* and allowing this love to lead me in the direction of wise choices that support my emotional and physical health. I am learning, firsthand, that it works. As I've built a strong connection to my body, I've naturally become drawn to the right foods, types of exercise, forms of self-care, and even healthcare practitioners. Yes, I now know that it all starts with love.

"Feeding your body well is such an important act of self-care," Louise continues, "especially while aging. It will support the natural changes we all experience as we get older. If you're going through menopause, for instance, and you're not feeding your body the right foods, you're going to have a much harder time. Eating good sources of protein and lots of vegetables (organic whenever possible), while saying affirmations like *This is a comfortable and easy time of my life, I am pleasantly surprised by how easily my body adapts to menopause,* or *I sleep well at night,* will make a big difference."

And what affirmations would you suggest for the man or woman who needs to love their body in spite of not liking what they see?

"Well, they could certainly start out by giving themselves messages like:

My body is such a good friend;
we have a great life together.

I listen to my body's messages and
take appropriate action.

I take the time to learn about how my body works and
what it needs nutritionally to be at optimal health.

The more I love my body, the healthier I feel.

"These affirmations will help get you started. And, if you really want to feel more connected to your body in a good way, you need to get in the habit of looking in the mirror every day and talking to it like a dear friend. You want to say things like:

Hi, body, thank you for being so healthy.

You are looking great today.

It is my joy to love you to perfect health.

You have the most beautiful eyes.

I love your beautiful shape.

I love every inch of you.

I love you dearly."

Experience has certainly taught me that speaking to your body in such a kind way will help you quiet the critical voice that judges you mercilessly. Over the years I'd read about using affirmations for loving the body in Louise's books, but when I first heard her *talk* about using them, I was touched by the level of warmth and intimacy in her voice. She wasn't just repeating the words; she was using a tone and inflection that made it clear we were to talk to ourselves like a kind and loving friend.

When I began to do this myself, my relationship with my body shifted dramatically. I felt the spirit of the words take hold in my heart. Each day as I looked in the mirror and spoke gently to myself, I felt the rough edges of judgment and harshness smooth out little by little. I could actually sense that my body was slowly becoming a dear friend instead of an embattled enemy. The trick was to do it *consistently.*

"Yes, yes, yes," Louise confirms. "It's all about the practice. Choose affirmations that feel most comfortable to you and start there. Know that your affirmations are creating new conditions and situations for you, and these habits will change your life. If we can make a habit of putting ourselves down, we can make a habit of building ourselves back up, too!"

So it goes back to what we keep saying throughout this book, that the most powerful steps really are the small, simple ones that start with our thinking. And we need to keep on practicing over time.

"Yes. And as you do, you need to look for the one little thing that shows you it's working—evidence that your consciousness is shifting. Then you want to focus on that success so you're inspired to keep going.

"You've done that yourself, Cheryl. You've done something that seemed silly to you at first—mirror work, for example—but then you started getting results. You wrote about that experience in your last book. And since we've been working together, I've seen it happen again with you. Pilates is a good example."

Louise is right. During one of our earlier visits, she invited me to join her for a private Pilates session, and since I'd always been curious about it, I agreed to give it a try. As someone who's lifted weights consistently for more than eight years, I was getting bored with my routine and wanted to find something new to add. I enjoyed the session with Louise so much that when I got home, I searched for a teacher and started taking weekly lessons myself.

In a short amount of time, I felt that I had made progress—the discovery of muscles I never knew existed and a feeling of inner strength that had me standing taller and feeling more alive. These were the outer signs that told me that what I was doing was working, but it was the success I felt on the *inside* that kept me going back.

Each time my teacher positioned me in front of a mirror so I could watch my form, I silently repeated positive affirmations to my body as I moved through the routines: *I love you, dear body, for holding me up; You are such a beautiful body; Thank you for being so flexible and cooperative today; I just love watching your strength and grace.* Not only was I strengthening and toning my outer muscles, I was building important inner muscles, too. My daily mirror work and my focus on self-love had led me to something that felt wonderful and right for my body.

"Isn't it interesting to see how Pilates came into your life?" Louise asks. "It was easy and effortless. You began to focus your attention on loving your body in a new way, and it just wandered in and you were willing to give it a try."

I guess I was in that state of mind you talk about, I tell her with a smile, the one that attracts exactly what we need and who we need at exactly the right time.

Now I'm doing Pilates three times a week and loving every minute of it!

"The important thing is that you were open to trying something new," Louise says. "Even if you hated it, I wanted you to have the experience—and if you said you didn't like it, that would have been fine. We need to be willing to try new things to find what works for our body. You start with one step and then take the next step and then the next. Before you know it, you started three blocks away and now you're here." She taps her finger on the table. "When you become more focused on the small steps you're taking instead of the end result—and you see that it's working—you feel good, and you continue to draw to you exactly what you need to take you where you want to go.

"Look at you, Cheryl. I suggest Pilates, you try it, and you discover you love it. Now you're doing it three times a week. Or you send love to Michael when you're about to argue over taking a wrong turn, and you feel the love, too. We try something, we see results, we realize our perspective has changed for the better, and it encourages us to continue. It doesn't really matter where you start as long as you're *willing* to start. You see, a lot of people will say: 'That's bullshit. That's just bullshit.' And you can't do anything if you think it's bullshit."

I could appreciate Louise's focus on recognizing what's working and taking our time to slowly develop new, self-loving habits. I used to get frustrated and feel defeated because I was always more focused on getting to the end result than experiencing the journey. Years ago during a conversation with a friend—another wise woman in her 80s—about trying to grow my speaking business, I expressed my frustration at how long it was taking to get where I wanted to go. I had been building my business for less than a year and was disappointed in my progress because I still hadn't booked a paid speech.

"You kids nowadays," she said, shaking her head. "You want success overnight. Whatever happened to the joy of mastering your craft? When I was growing up, people took years to achieve the kind of success you want yesterday, and they actually enjoyed the process. Slow down, my friend. It will make the ride much more interesting."

I did my best to relax and take this advice. However, there I was again years later, pacing back and forth in my kitchen, complaining to my husband about how long it was taking me to build my coaching practice—a brand-new profession launched just a year and a half earlier.

Louise's message was falling on well-seasoned ears, and I knew it was important. Our culture has trained us to focus on the quick, end result—losing ten pounds in a week or getting a flat stomach overnight with the right fiber supplement. We want *big* success, *big* changes, *big* results immediately!

"Yes," Louise agrees. "Big, big, big . . . and lots of suffering in the process. We want to enjoy what we do. You've been doing Pilates for a while now—and, yes, you've kept the commitment, but it's also important that you're enjoying yourself. That's lovely. And your body is changing in a very positive way. We need to stop focusing on healing the perceived problem. Instead, we want to focus on making small, positive changes that make us feel better along the way. That's what makes loving ourselves, loving our bodies, and the process of aging easier and more joyful—small, positive changes."

Speaking of aging, I ask Louise if we could talk more about the subject. I wonder what she's been most concerned about as she's gotten older.

"Well, some people are concerned about losing their youthful looks. But years ago I used to worry about losing my mental faculties. I must have received some kind of message early in my childhood that planted this fear in my mind. It's long gone now, and today I know enough to keep my mind healthy with good thoughts and good nutrition. When your diet is a mess, you set yourself up for trouble as you age. My concern now would be about losing my health. That's why I take good care of myself."

We all face different challenges as we age. As I approached 50, I went through my share of looking in the mirror and feeling sad or distressed about new wrinkles or sagging skin, but what concerned me more was something else—the idea of losing energy. I've always been a woman with lots of energy who prided herself on accomplishing goals and getting things done at home and at work. As I began to notice my energy waning a bit, I chalked it up to getting older and started to worry. Was this the beginning of the end of my productive years? Would I have to work even harder to eat well and exercise to keep my energy levels up? Or did I need to surrender to the reality that we all slow down as we age?

In the last year, I've come to understand energy in a new way. Yes, I need to support myself with good self-care, but I can also embrace the gift that aging has to offer: the presence of mind to slow down so I can use my energy in a more intentional way. Age and experience have given me permission to spend my precious energy on the treasured priorities that matter most—my self-care, my significant relationships, the alone time I need to feel spiritually rejuvenated, and forms of creative expression that feed my soul.

There's nothing like a ticking clock to help you worry less about the mundane details of life, or about what others think. That's the real gift of aging. That, and the fact that I've become far more interested in being open to Life's direction—responding to what shows up—rather than trying to direct Life with my old striving, succeeding, make-it-happen self. While I may not have the same youthful appearance of ten years ago, I have a new kind of beauty—the beauty of wisdom.

"The funny thing is that now you'll have fewer wrinkles," Louise tells me with a giggle. "Let's face it, people who are really worried about aging and how they look become very tense. When we make peace with aging, we're more concerned with being happy and comfortable with ourselves.

"You're not going to be 20, 30, 40, or 50 again; you're going to be where you are. If you were to look back at photos of yourself ten years ago, you'd think, *God, I looked good*. But when you were that age, I'm sure you never thought you looked good enough. We're much better looking than we think we are anyway, and we need to appreciate that now."

I'm also aware of being kinder and gentler to myself, I say. And I have a hunch that I'm a nicer person to be around.

"I notice the same thing now that we've been working on this book," Louise comments. "The other day I was leaving a meeting, and when I attempted to drive back the way I'd come, there was a truck in the way and I couldn't take the same route. So I had to go around and around, and I didn't know where I was but knew where I wanted to go. In the past this was something I would have been irritated about, but instead, I kept saying to myself, 'It's okay, it's all right. You know, you've never been on this road before, and it's a pretty road. Just keep going, and you'll get to where you want to go.' And suddenly it was, 'Oh, here I am! I'm back on the road I want.'"

Are you always observing your thoughts and actions and making adjustments? Is that why you seem to have such a curiosity about life?

"I *do* have a curiosity about life, and it has helped me stay young at heart. Very much so. I love to take classes, I love to study, and I love to learn new things. I'm waiting for something interesting to come my way now so I can take a new class. I also listen to people a lot—what they say, how they express themselves. I'm very curious about people as well as how I talk to myself. The more we listen to ourselves and make positive changes based on what we discover, the more interesting life becomes."

Listening to Louise's wisdom, I'm convinced that this insatiable curiosity of hers is directly responsible for why she's aged so well. When we love learning—when we're committed to our own personal growth and then back up that commitment with action—

we stay engaged with life in a purposeful and fulfilling way. We feel more connected to ourselves, each other, and the larger source of energy called Life. Things seem to flow as we live in alignment with our essence, the part of us that is timeless and endless.

I wonder what beliefs have served Louise as she's aged, and she gives me a big smile. "I believe that I am a big, strong, healthy girl with lots of good energy. I am so pleased to have the energy I do, to be able to live the life I do, and to enjoy the company of fabulous friends. I believe that Life loves me. I believe that I am safe at all times. I believe that only good experiences lie before me, and I bless others and know that Life blesses and prospers me. I know that all is well in my world.

"I also believe that laughter is more important than worrying about wrinkles. I find myself laughing more. Fewer things bother me. As a matter of fact, I feel freer than I did when I was a child. It's as though my good thoughts have returned me to a state of innocence that feels blissful. I kid myself and make jokes more often these days. I have cultivated a mental outlook that allows me to see life from the most positive advantage. This positive, loving, grateful, joyous outlook attracts to me the greatest life—and that's why this is the best decade so far."

And what about your spiritual beliefs? What role do they play in your life now?

"It's interesting. I grew up with absolutely no religion at all, and it was probably one of the best things that happened to me. I didn't have to unlearn anything. When I was introduced to the metaphysical world at the Church of Religious Science, it made so much sense to me—the belief that we are all expressions of Divine Intelligence, and when we align ourselves with this intelligence, we can create a desired outcome. I used to go to church a lot, and I absorbed the teachings. But today my garden is my church. I go out and work there, and I find peace. If there's a fantastic minister or teacher speaking nearby, I may want to go and hear them, but I've heard a lot already. Now I live it."

It's time for Louise and me to attend an authors' party hosted by Hay House for the team speaking at the conference. However, she has one more important piece of advice about health and aging to share with me.

"We need to make touch more of a habit, too. We all need more hugs. While I know many people can't afford bodywork, we can always afford hugs. We used to do this during our Hayride groups, and it always made people smile. Hugs will keep you young and happy." And with that, she stands up, walks over to me, and gives me a big hug.

As I feel the strength in her arms and the smile in her heart, I think, *Yup, I'd say that's one fine way to make aging a whole lot easier.*

CHAPTER SEVEN

The End of the Movie

As I step out of the shower, I feel the weight of melancholy pulling at my chest. There's a sadness I can't explain. I sit down on the edge of the tub and give presence to it—allow it to live and breathe within me. Wait for it to deliver its wisdom. With each slow, deep breath, the answer begins to surface. Spring is in the ethers, and my winter of writing is coming to an end. It's almost time to say good-bye to this book.

I know the routine. As the ending of a book creeps up on me, I tend to simultaneously rush to finish it and slow down to savor the process one last time. This is my final chapter, and finishing is always bittersweet. But there's something more. . . .

I realize that I'm also anxious about a dear friend who is seriously ill. I'm afraid for him, for me, for us. I towel-dry my hair, brush on a bit of mascara, and glide some gloss across my lips. I need to get dressed. Louise and I are in downtown Vancouver for an event, and we're meeting for breakfast in half an hour (and she's always early). This time, I have an agenda.

We sit at a quiet table in the back of the restaurant at our hotel. The ritual has now become second nature: I sit down, immediately take out my iPhone and press RECORD, and I unpack my notes. Sitting in front of Louise, I feel a bit wobbly, vulnerable. I'm doing my best to hold back the tears, but I can't help but feel transparent in her presence. She can see that something is wrong but doesn't say anything. Instead, she just stares into my eyes and waits for me to speak.

I have a dear friend who is seriously ill, I tell her, and I'm afraid he might be dying. While I want to be positive, I can't help but worry about whether or not he'll make it, and I don't know how to talk to him about it. I know you've had plenty of experience with illness and death, and I just need to know what to do.

"You *love* him," she responds immediately. "And you make it a good experience. When people are in trouble, I always concentrate on a few things. First, I focus on who they are as a person, not on their disease. I like to remind them of how wonderful they are—

how funny, thoughtful, wise, or kind. And I often bring up favorite memories from our time together. Most important, I allow them to lead the process. We need to respect where people are. I simply ask how they feel in any given situation, and let their answer direct where our conversation will go from there."

As I listen to Louise speak, reluctant tears spill from my eyes, and she reaches into her bag for a tissue. "You never know where we're going on these trips, do you?" she notes with a smile, tucking the tissue into my hand. "It's hard when this happens."

I know we must think positive, but—

"But wait," she interrupts. "Death is not negative. Death is a positive step in life. We're all going to do it. You're upset because you just don't want your friend to do it at this time."

Or in a way that's painful, I admit.

"Yes, it's important to be sure that our loved ones are pain free. I remember when my mother was ready to go. She was 91 and became very sick, and they wanted to perform a monumental operation on her. I said, 'No way! You're not going to put this woman through something like that at her age. Just keep her out of pain.' That was the top priority—keep her out of pain and let her drift off. And that's what happened. Over the next several days, she drifted in and out of consciousness. She would drift out and come back talking about relatives, and then drift off again and come back with another story. She didn't have pain, which was so important to me.

"We're all going to leave this life at some point, Cheryl, and I don't think there's anything to be afraid of. You see, I wasn't raised with hell and damnation. I mean, I lived it . . . but since I wasn't raised with that concept, I'm not afraid of death. I don't think I'm going to hell. I've done that already."

This last statement was said in such a matter-of-fact way that it could only be recited by someone who had transcended a painful past. I nod, smile, and wipe my cheeks.

"We need to address the vast array of stuff we're taught about death," Louise continues. "If your parents went to a church filled with messages of hellfire and damnation, you could be very frightened of death. You'll wonder, *Have I been good enough, and if not, am I going to burn forever?* And if you think you're going to burn forever, then you'll be scared shitless of dying.

"No wonder so many people are terrified of death. A lot of religions share that message in one form or another—that you're a sinner and you have to behave or you're going to pay for it when you die. You may not be burned in hell, but you *will* pay. In that way, death becomes quite scary."

I think about the concept of hell and damnation, and recall my own childhood experience. I was very familiar with the idea of heaven and hell, as well as something in between—purgatory or limbo. I was raised to believe that you went to heaven if you were a good, rule-abiding Catholic, and to hell if you were not. Purgatory and limbo were the in-between states for those who needed to atone for their sins, or for children who had not received the sacrament of baptism.

As a little girl, I used to kneel by my bed before going to sleep, repeating the words *Jesus, Mary, and Joseph* as many times as I could to help move souls from purgatory to heaven. I hated the idea of people being stuck in a place where they were frightened and alone. Fortunately, as I matured and began to explore a variety of religious and spiritual traditions, I went on to trade in the concept of hell for a personal belief that death is merely a transition point that reunites us all with our Creator in a state of love, compassion, and forgiveness.

Are you afraid of death at this point in your life? I ask Louise.

"No. I don't want to go right now because there are things I want to do, but I'm going to say that throughout my entire life. We all will. There's always one more thing to do—a child's wedding to attend, a baby ready to be born, or a book to write. I also have this very strong feeling that we arrive in the middle of the movie, and we leave in the middle of the movie. The movie is continuous. We enter and we exit. All of us do that. There's no wrong time or right time, there's just *our* time—it was our time to be born and our time to go."

I think about the idea of leaving in the middle of the movie and agree that it is the hard part of death—never having a "buttoned-up time" to go.

As Louise explains, "I believe that long before we arrive, the soul makes the choice to experience certain lessons—lessons about loving each other and ourselves. When we learn the lesson of love, we may leave with joy. There is no need for pain or suffering. We know that next time, wherever we choose to incarnate, we will take all of the love with us."

So the question is, then, how to make peace with leaving in the middle of the movie. The problem, as I see it, is that we are so uncomfortable with death. We don't talk about it. We don't prepare for it. We don't even allow ourselves to think about our fears and concerns. We live in a culture that avoids the topic altogether. Instead, we wait until we're up against a serious illness and forced to make important decisions under pressure—for loved ones or ourselves—and then wonder why it's so frightening and painful.

To make peace with leaving, we first need to be willing to address the issue. We need to face the awkwardness and uncomfortable feelings associated with death by looking fear in the eye. When we do, we discover what that fear has to teach us.

I certainly ignored anything having to do with death until my early 30s, when I had the privilege of going through the process of dying in a conscious way with someone I cared about. Her name was Lucy, and she was in her 80s. Lucy had a house filled with lifelong treasures, a wise mind, and a big heart . . . but no family. During a hospital visit for a bad chest cold, she was told that she was dying of cancer, and she promptly asked me to help her get her affairs in order. My first reaction was, *No way! I have no interest whatsoever in stepping into that minefield.* However, after further discussion, my compassion (and guilt) got the better of me, and I reluctantly agreed.

What unfolded over the next three months was nothing short of a miracle. One by one, Lucy and I reviewed the treasures in her home and made plans to give them to specific people. I became intimately familiar with her life, her loves, and her desires for how to end her life. I made her a promise that I would follow through on her wishes, both while she was dying and once she was gone.

On the night of Lucy's death, I had given a speech and was home tucked in bed when something told me to get up and make the hour-long trip to see her. Knowing enough to trust my gut, I did what it instructed and drove to the hospital. Once there, I found my friend unconscious, in a private room, stationed with a loving and compassionate nurse who assured me that she could hear everything I said.

For almost an hour I sat by Lucy's side, reviewing the instructions she had given me about her end-of-life planning. I talked them through, out loud, as she lay before me. I assured her that all was in order and that it was okay to make the transition to a more peaceful place. Was I frightened? You bet. But I was also prepared.

While I was looking at her beautiful face, she suddenly woke up, looked directly into my eyes, gave me a big smile, and took her last breath. In that moment, something significant shifted. Death and I had become intimate friends.

I sat by Lucy's side that night for quite a while after she passed, staring at her face, her hands, and her lifeless body, contemplating this scary thing we call death. But I wasn't scared. Instead, I felt safe, touched in a tender and profound way, and surprised by how natural the actual process turned out to be. Yes, I would miss my friend, but from this new perspective, death wasn't the silent monster I had made it out to be—a bogeyman who needed to be locked away, only to be let out at the last possible moment. It was a gentle state of release and surrender, the completion of a promise.

"You see, you've been through one death experience, and you know it's not going to kill you," Louise says to me now. "It turns out to be more beautiful than awful when we approach it with love and proper planning. It can be a nightmare, however, if you're not prepared.

"A year ago, after a good friend of mine became seriously ill, I thought a lot about my own death. He was a minister who was so good with people who were facing the end of their lives. He knew just the right things to say and do. He was fabulous at handling death. But when it came to be *his* time to go, things were very different. He was a bloody pain in the ass. He was constantly whining and moaning, complaining that this was wrong or that was wrong. If you sat him down, he wanted to get up; and if you got him up, he wanted to sit down. Pretty soon, everybody was pissed at him. As I watched what went on, I wondered why he couldn't do for himself what he had done for others."

After pausing for a moment, she goes on. "Seeing my friend die a difficult death showed me the wrong way to do it. So many people loved him, yet so many of us ended up wanting to punch him. He wouldn't allow us to love him. I think he was scared and hadn't dealt with a lot of stuff."

So seeing how he made the transition made you think about how you'd want to make the transition yourself, I say. How would you want to do it?

"First, I would allow people to love me as much as they wanted to. I would allow people to take care of me. I would allow people to make it a wonderful experience. Although I'd probably be comforting *them*. Now that, to me, would be the ideal situation: allowing others to love me while comforting them at the same time. Either that or I'd like to simply go to sleep one night after a lovely party and not wake up."

We both laugh in acknowledgment of the peace and simplicity of this idea.

"When it's my turn to leave," Louise clarifies, "I want it to be a conscious process, and I want to be focused on how I can make it as comfortable as possible. Since I went through that experience with my friend, I made a decision to put two people in charge of my passing—one who will make decisions related to my body, and one who will support my emotional and spiritual comfort. When it's my time to go, I will now have someone with me who is familiar and comfortable with the dying process."

The idea of handpicking people to support us emotionally and spiritually, as well as physically, when we come to the end of our lives is a revolutionary thought. How much better would you feel knowing that you were safe, comfortable, and pain free, surrounded by those who were well prepared to support your needs and transition? Imagine thinking about—I mean really considering—the ideal circumstances of your death. . . .

Because we don't talk about death, later in life we end up feeling thrust into a medical system that's charged with treating the body but not necessarily the heart or mind. Suddenly, we may find ourselves in the hospital being poked and prodded, at the mercy of whoever happens to be on duty. Feeling frightened and unprepared to make smart choices that honor our emotional, physical, and spiritual health, we pay the high cost of not having the loving and caring support that we deserve in place.

Louise's willingness to plan her transition is a gutsy, profound act of self-care. Having the eyes, ears, and mind of someone we trust can mean the difference between a peaceful ending and a disaster. So I had to ask her what guidelines she used to choose the two people she's asked to support her transition. Were there certain qualities she looked for or steps she's put in place to direct the process?

"I've chosen two people I trust to be there for me at the end of my life," she replies. "They know what I want, what it takes for me to be comfortable, and they have agreed to abide by my wishes. I know them well, and I trust their experience. They both know their particular areas of expertise so well that I won't need to give them specific instructions. One gentleman has helped many, many people go through the end of their lives, and the other is a health-care practitioner who knows my body and my health needs. I can trust them to do what they say they're going to do, and that's the important thing."

So it's the planning that contributes to the peace? Facing death reduces our fear?

"I must say that while far too many young men died with AIDS at the time I was working with them, a lot of them died with peace. We talked about death, and we faced it together. I remember one man, David Soloman, who allowed us to perform his funeral in front of him. He knew he only had a few days left, and he came to our meeting in a wheelchair."

I see tears spring to Louise's eyes, and it's my turn to hunt for a tissue. "We said all the wonderful things we would have said at his funeral to his face," she tells me. "It was a beautiful experience for us all. We wanted to make it a peaceful, loving, and comforting time for him. And we did."

What a beautiful ritual, I say, as I look into her eyes.

"I used to do this silly thing with all of the guys. I would talk about reincarnation and tell them that I would look for them again in the faces of babies. I used to mimic what I would do: 'Is that you, David Soloman? Is that you in there? Have you come back to see us? You look so cute.' And they would all laugh and laugh."

I, too, laugh out loud as she relives this story. Then I ask if she feels as if working with these men with AIDS was some of her most fulfilling work.

"It was incredible. It was incredible," she repeats. "Astrologically, that's when Pluto went over my sun, a time when most people struggle terribly because there are all sorts of lessons about death. But I got the ultimate lesson. I was so busy dealing with the men that I didn't have any time to worry about myself. And the simpler I was and the less I did, the more they would tell me what a wonderful meeting it was.

"Sometimes I would just sit there, do a little opening prayer and meditation, choose someone to speak—and when they were done, choose someone else. And at the end of the meeting, we would do healing triads. Someone would lie down, and then one person would sit at the head and another at the feet, touching the body of the person in front of them, while I led a meditation with music. And then we'd switch so everyone got a chance to receive the love. The simple things meant the most to them."

Are there affirmations you've used for dealing with death?

"Yes, we want to use those that deal with belief systems about what's on the other side. It's important to notice whether there is a frightened little kid inside who remembers hell and damnation. We need to do affirmations to heal those beliefs so that death won't be as frightening."

Louise offers some that she's used over the years:

At the end of this lifetime, I look forward to being reconnected with my loved ones on the other side.

I make my journey to the other side of this life with joy and ease and peace in my heart.

I am so excited to see loved ones at the end of this journey.

I see only love and peace on the other side of this stage of my life.

Only good lies before me. I am safe, and I am loved.

"It's easier to go if you feel comforted," she says. "If you go feeling that it's going to be a good thing, then you're not terrified."

And since we don't know what's on the other side . . .

"That's right. No one knows. We have people who have very strong beliefs who will tell us what is true, but no one really knows. We want to encourage people to think about and prepare for the end of their lives in a comforting way. It doesn't matter what age we are, this is important to do. I could outlive the people I've chosen to care for me, and then I'm sure that Life would give me another option. I've been rescued from lots of things. I might have gone through shit, but I was always saved."

Why do you think that is?

"Well, I suppose there's a possibility that it's because I had important work ahead of me, so I always came out of a scrape. I've always been the kind of person who takes risks. After all, when you reach out to Life, Life always seems to reach back."

Louise certainly does reach out to Life. At the end of what I imagine to be our last meeting, I walk back to my room feeling full of love and deep admiration for this life-changing experience. How blessed I am to have spent so much time with such an extraordinary woman. As I slide my key down through the hotel-room lock, I know my life will never be the same. I also know something else deep in my bones: *Life certainly does love me.*

Several days later, after returning home from our trip to Vancouver and reviewing my notes, I think about how I might end this book. Rather than struggle to find the right words, I surrender and allow the perfect ending to find me.

The answer comes a few days later, in the form of an e-mail from Louise. It's a letter she's found from years ago, sent to a young man who was dying of AIDS. It couldn't be more perfect:

> *Dearest One,*
>
> *Here are some thoughts I have about the perfectly normal, natural process of leaving the planet—a process we will all go through. The more peaceful we can be with this experience, the easier it will be. Here's what I know:*
>
> *We are always safe*
> *It is only change*
> *From the moment we are born*
> *We are preparing to be embraced*
> *by the Light once more*

Position yourself for maximum peace
Angels surround you
They are guiding you each step of the way

However you choose your exit
Will be perfect for you

Everything will happen in
The perfect time-space sequence

This is a time for joy
and for rejoicing
You are on your way home

As we all are.

Collected Affirmations

For healing:

I love myself, and I forgive myself.

I forgive myself for allowing my [anger, resentment, fear, or what have you] *to harm my body.*

I deserve to be healed.

I am worthy of being healed.

My body knows how to heal itself.

I cooperate with my body's nutritional needs.

I feed my body delicious, healthy foods.

I love every inch of my body.

I see cool, clear water flowing through my body washing away all impurities.

My healthy cells grow stronger every day.

I trust Life to support my healing in every way.

Every hand that touches my body is a healing hand.

My doctors are amazed by how quickly my body is healing.

Every day in every way I am growing healthier and healthier.

I love myself.

I am safe.

Life loves me.

I am healed and whole.

When you first wake up and open your eyes:

Good morning bed, thank you for being so comfortable, I love you.

Darling [your name], *this is a blessed day.*

All is well. I have time for everything I need to do today.

Looking in the bathroom mirror:

Good morning, [your name]. *I love you. I really, really love you.*

There are great experiences coming our way today.

You look wonderful.

You have the best smile.

Your makeup [or hair] *looks perfect.*

You are my ideal woman [or man].

We are having a terrific day today.

I love you dearly.

In the shower:

I love my body, and my body loves me.

It is such a pleasure to take a shower.

The water feels so good.

I am grateful for the people who designed and built this shower.

My life is so blessed.

I am showered with good thoughts all day long!

Using the bathroom:

I easily release all that my body no longer needs.

Intake, assimilation, and elimination are all in Divine right order.

Getting dressed:

I love my closet.

It is so easy for me to get dressed.

I always pick the best thing to wear.

I am comfortable in my clothing.

I trust my inner wisdom to pick the perfect outfit for me.

In the kitchen:

Hello, kitchen, you are my nourishment center. I appreciate you!

You and all your appliances help me so much in easily preparing delicious, nutritious meals.

There is such an abundance of good, healthy food in my fridge.

I can easily make a delicious, nutritious meal.

You help me be cheerful.

I love you.

DURING MEALS:

I am so grateful to have this wonderful food.

I bless this meal/food with love.

I love selecting foods that are nutritious and delicious.

The whole family is enjoying this meal.

Mealtime is laughter time. Laughter is good for the digestion.

Planning healthy meals is a joy.

My body loves the way I choose the perfect foods for every meal.

I am so fortunate that I can choose healthy foods for my family.

We are all now nourished in preparation for the day before us.

In this house, all our meals are harmonious.

We gather together with great joy and love.

Mealtimes are happy times.

The kids love to try new foods.

My body heals and strengthens with every bite I take.

When driving:

I am surrounded by good drivers, and I send love into all the cars around me.

My ride is easy and effortless.

My drive goes smoothly, and more quickly than I expect.

I feel comfortable in the car.

I know this will be a beautiful drive to the office [or to school, the store, or the like].

I bless my car with love.

I send love to every person on the road.

Throughout the day:

I love my life.

I love this day.

Life loves me.

I love it when the sun shines.

It is wonderful to feel the love in my heart.

Everything I do brings me joy.

Changing my thoughts is easy and comfortable.

It is a joy to speak to myself in kind and loving ways.

This is a glorious day, and every experience is a joyous adventure.

At work:

I work in creative collaboration with smart, inspiring people on projects that contribute to the healing of the world.

I bless this job with love.

I have a wonderful relationship with everyone at work, including ________________.

I am surrounded by wonderful co-workers.

All my co-workers are just a delight to be with.

We have so much fun together.

I have a wonderful relationship with my boss.

I always love where I work. I have the best jobs. I am always appreciated.

I release this job to the next person, who will be so glad to be here.

I accept a job that uses all my creative talents and abilities.

This job is deeply fulfilling, and it is a joy for me to go to work each day.

I work for people who appreciate me.

The building where I work is light, bright, and airy; and filled with a feeling of enthusiasm.

My new job is in the perfect location and I earn good money, for which I am deeply grateful.

When arriving back home:

Good evening, house, I am back home.

I am so glad to be here. I love you.

Let us have a great evening together.

I am looking forward to seeing my family.

We have a lovely time together tonight.

The kids whiz through their homework in no time.

Dinner seems to make itself.

At the end of the day (say in the bathroom mirror):

Thank you, Life, for this day.

I am grateful for each experience.

I take this moment to breathe and let go.

I bless with love all those I have encountered this day. All is well in my world.

Going to bed:

Hi, bed, I am so glad to be with you. Thank you for welcoming me again.

I relax and release the day, and I allow you to comfort me.

All my dreams are peaceful.

I awaken tomorrow refreshed and looking forward to the new day.

I know Life loves me. Good night.

As you drift off to sleep, repeat, "Life loves me, and I am safe."

To support health and loving the body:

This is a comfortable and easy time of my life.

I am pleasantly surprised by how easily my body adapts to menopause.

I sleep well at night.

My body is such a good friend; we have a great life together.

I listen to my body's messages and take appropriate action.

I take the time to learn about how my body works and what it needs nutritionally to be at optimal health.

The more I love my body, the healthier I feel.

Hi, body, thank you for being so healthy.

You are looking great today.

It is my joy to love you to perfect health.

You have the most beautiful eyes.

I love your beautiful shape.

I love every inch of you.

I love you dearly.

I love you, dear body, for holding me up.

You are such a beautiful body.

Thank you for being so flexible and cooperative today.

I just love watching your strength and grace.

When facing difficulties:

I release this incident with love; it is over and done.

I look with expectation to my next moment, which is fresh and new.

Only good experiences lie before me.

I am greeted with love wherever I go.

I love Life, and Life loves me.

All is well, and so am I.

All is well. Everything is working out for my highest good. Out of this situation only good will come. I am safe.

I enjoy a peaceful resolution to this problem. The uncomfortable situation is resolved quickly, and everyone feels content with the outcome.

I release all drama from my life and now get energy from peace.

For prosperity:

I prosper wherever I turn.

My income is constantly increasing.

I bless and prosper everyone in my world, and everyone in my world blesses and prospers me.

Life loves me, and all my needs are met at all times.

I gratefully accept all the good I have in my life now.

Life loves me and provides for me.

I trust Life to take care of me.

I am worthy of abundance.

Life always provides for my needs.

Abundance flows into my life in surprising ways every day.

To prepare for the end of life:

At the end of this lifetime, I look forward to being reconnected with my loved ones on the other side.

I make my journey to the other side of this life with joy and ease and peace in my heart.

I am so excited to see loved ones at the end of this journey.

I see only love and peace on the other side of this stage of my life.

Only good lies before me. I am safe, and I am loved.

About the Authors

Louise Hay was an inspirational teacher who educated millions since the 1984 publication of her bestseller *You Can Heal Your Life*, which has more than 50 million copies in print worldwide. Renowned for demonstrating the power of affirmations to bring about positive change, Louise was the author of more than 30 books for adults and children, including the bestsellers *The Power Is Within You* and *Heal Your Body*. In addition to her books, Louise produced numerous audio and video programs, card decks, online courses, and other resources for leading a healthy, joyous, and fulfilling life.

Websites:
www.louisehay.com, www.healyourlife.com,
and **www.facebook.com/louiselhay**

Cheryl Richardson is the *New York Times* best-selling author of *Take Time for Your Life, Life Makeovers, Stand Up for Your Life, The Unmistakable Touch of Grace,* and *The Art of Extreme Self-Care*. She leads large web communities at **www.cherylrichardson.com** and **www.facebook.com/cherylrichardson**, which are dedicated to helping people around the world improve their quality of life.

Hay House Titles of Related Interest

YOU CAN HEAL YOUR LIFE, the movie,
starring Louise Hay & Friends
(available as a 1-DVD program, an expanded 2-DVD set,
and an online streaming video)
Learn more at **www.hayhouse.com/louise-movie**

THE SHIFT, the movie,
starring Dr. Wayne W. Dyer
(available as a 1-DVD program, an expanded 2-DVD set,
and an online streaming video)
Learn more at **www.hayhouse.com/the-shift-movie**

The Age of Miracles: *Embracing the New Midlife,*
by Marianne Williamson

The Body Knows . . . How to Stay Young:
Healthy-Aging Secrets from a Medical Intuitive,
by Caroline Sutherland

A Daily Dose of Sanity: *A Five-Minute Soul Recharge for Every Day of the Year,* by Alan Cohen

A Deep Breath of Life: *Daily Inspiration for Heart-Centered Living,* by Alan Cohen

How Your Mind Can Heal Your Body,
by David Hamilton

***It's Not about the Horse:** It's about Overcoming Fear and Self-Doubt,*
by Wyatt Webb, with Cindy Pearlman

***The Law of Attraction:** The Basics of the Teachings of Abraham™,*
by Esther and Jerry Hicks

***Seeds of Freedom:** Cultivating a Life That Matters,*
by Heather Marie Wilson

***Shift Happens!:** How to Live an Inspired Life . . . Starting Right Now!,*
by Robert Holden, Ph.D.

***Visions, Trips, and Crowded Rooms:** Who and What You See Before You Die,*
by David Kessler

We hope you enjoyed this Hay House book. If you'd like to receive our online catalog featuring additional information on Hay House books and products, or if you'd like to find out more about the Hay Foundation, please contact:

HAY HOUSE

Hay House Publishers (India) Pvt Ltd
Muskaan Complex, Plot No. 3,
B-2, Vasant Kunj, New Delhi 110 070
Phone: +91 11 41761620
www.hayhouse.co.in

—

Published in the United States by:
Hay House LLC, P.O. Box 5100, Carlsbad, CA 92018-5100
(760) 31-7695 or (800) 654-5126
www.hayhouse.com® • www.hayfoundation.org

Published in Australia by:
Hay House Australia Publishing Pty Ltd
18/36 Ralph St., Alexandria NSW 2015
Phone: +61 (02) 9669 4299
www.hayhouse.com.au

Published in the United Kingdom by:
Hay House UK Ltd
1st Floor, Crawford Corner,
91–93 Baker Street, London W1U 6QQ
Phone: +44 (0)20 3927 7290
www.hayhouse.co.uk

—